PASTORAL STRESS

sources of tension

resources for transformation

Anthony G. Pappas

An Alban Institute Publication

The Publications Program of The Alban Institute is assisted by a grant from
Trinity Church, New York City.

Library of Congress Catalog Card Number 95-75682
ISBN 1-56699-150-1

TABLE OF CONTENTS

PREFACE

Few people will read a book about stress as an abstract exercise. Most of us, myself especially, seek to gain a greater understanding of stress from within the midst of it. We experience many types of stress: stress from familial relations, stress relative to vocational choice, existential angst, etc. In this volume we will address one particular category of stress: the stress pastors experience in the performance of the pastoral function. Of course, stress is an oozy kind of thing and pastoral stress may spill over or be spilled into by many other aspects of stress. (Note: If you experience chronic stress or acute stress to the point of depression or thoughts of suicide, consult your physician or a counsellor straightaway.)

While I make no claim to address and eliminate all sources of stress, let me offer a few general strategies with which to respond to generic stress:

1. **Get physical exercise.** Stress has a way of closing down the body. Exercise opens up and energizes the body. Endorphins are released, our body's natural stress fighters. Oxygen levels are increased through exercise. Muscle tone is enhanced. One just feels better with appropriate amounts of exercise. While exercise alone won't eliminate stress, it is a strategic response that allows a more constructive approach to the stress one is experiencing.

2. **Develop or utilize a support system.** It is always helpful to have friends, colleagues, and relatives with whom one can share one's struggles. There is a catharsis involved in sharing one's stresses. Oftentimes new insights are gained simply through the process of articulation. A

feeling of personal support can sometimes strengthen one enough to fight on. And, of course, their responses coming from another, often more detached, perspective, can be just the key to unlocking the puzzle of the next step forward.

3. **Take time alone.** Go on a personal retreat. A morning, a day, an overnight without an agenda can allow the voice of the Lord to filter through the barricades of busyness. This can be a scary thing to do. I know that I collude with my own busyness to keep these times to a minimum. Spiritual *discipline* is aptly named. The story is told of the disciple who questioned his spiritual director as to why he was to go to the beach before dawn and face east; he couldn't cause the sun to rise. No, replied the master, but at least there you will be ready when it does rise. Take time alone.

4. **Change things.** Change your activities, change your pace, change your focus. It can be very frustrating to stay in the pain and experience no forward motion. This frustration can add to the original stress. When I've had it with my boards, I go out and chop firewood. Certain parishioners have got me through many a winter! Some suggest working on your stress until you are dead-ended, then give it up and do something totally different. Often one's conscious mind is the obstacle. Changing one's activity or focus allows the unconscious mind (often, the instrument of God's voice) to kick in. The change of pace will be refreshing and so will a spontaneous insight "out of the blue."

5. **Take care of yourself.** Eat. Sleep. Pray. Share. Go gently with yourself. Do upbuilding things. Do fun things. Goof off. Your destruction is not the point of stress. Stress requires health and builds health. Keep yourself healthy.

6. **Wrestle while you work.** It is work to wrest the blessing from stress. Stress is an energy you experience in a situation. All stress is an invitation to self-examination and situational analysis. To turn stress into strength, be prepared for the work of increasing self-realization and increasing environmental competence. At least you won't be expecting a picnic!

In the following pages I will offer a number of specific tools for the work of self-realization and environmental competence. Not every tool will be appropriate for you at all times, but may God bless you as you do use the ones that fit.

Tony Pappas
Block Island, 1995

CHAPTER 1

Toward a Constructive
Perspective on Pastoral Stress

Introduction

Everybody experiences stress. Some experience it as a blessing, some as a curse. For some stress is eustress (good stress, motivating, challenging); for some stress is simply distress. I do not believe that the way you or I handle stress is preordained and unchangeable. Rather, our ways of coping with stress are learned. If we so desire, we can change the way we respond to stress. This book invites us who are pastors—or lay persons, denomination people and seminary professors who care about the well-being of pastors—to look at our stress response patterns. It offers a fresh way to perceive stress and multiple handles on transforming "distress" to "eustress." But first, let me share how and why this book came to be.

A Creation Story

Everything that is came into being. There is a story behind every becoming. The Creation Story of this book started with a letter.

Now that's peculiar, I thought. Lead a pastors' retreat. OK. In South Dakota. Fine. On the topic of "Life in the Fishbowl." Hmmmm. Next month. Next month??!! That's crazy. I can't possibly get a week's worth of presentations together on a new topic in a month! It's too bad, too. It would be fun to focus on the tensions that occur in a close and closed environment and how to deal with them. Oh, well . . .

As I reread the letter, formulating a thanks-but-no-thanks response, I noticed one very small but significant fact: the date. The retreat was not next month; it was next year, thirteen months ahead! I accepted, disclaiming to be an expert in the area. That's OK, they answered. Anybody who can survive on a small island for a decade and a half must know something. It's possible, I acknowledged, wondering just what it was I was supposed to know.

In that invitation the American Baptist pastors of South Dakota offered an opportunity that evolved into a rich blessing for me. For I now had a mandate to target tension, to concentrate on conflict, to stand behind myself, look over my own shoulder, and see how stress comes and where it goes. I had license to objectify life in the fishbowl. No longer would issues simply arise, be dealt with, and that was that. Now I would follow myself around with a mental notebook. Where did that issue come from? Who saw it? How was it responded to? What resulted? What other alternatives existed? Maybe the unexamined life was not worth living, but I was about to find out if the examined one was! So my examination of life in the fishbowl began. I was on the lookout for stress, tension, and conflict.

Personally, I wasn't so sure. I am a pretty mellow person, with broad goals and flexible strategies, or so I thought. And our congregation is big on fellowship, warm and loving. Where would all this conflict come from? How was I going to fill a week in South Dakota? My anxiety started to rise. Ah, good, my first instance of stress! But that didn't count for life *in* the fishbowl. I calmed down and continued my stakeout. In that year of stress search I learned three things about myself, my congregation, and the nature of things.

The first was that there was trouble right here in River City! I had thought life in my congregation to be basically rosy and harmonious. Oh, yes, there had been a few "incidents," but I had taken them to be the exception rather than the rule. Now I began to see that much of the rosiness was the afterglow of little flare-ups, bruised egos, frustrated desires, disappointed expectations, conflicts in goals, differences in values. Tension fairly seeped out of the woodwork! I had thought of our congregation as a ship; we might face rough seas occasionally, but "steady as she goes" described our movement. Now I came to see us as a person walking toward a distant destination. Sure, we were moving forward, but it was through a process of continuous alternation between balance and imbalance.

The second thing I learned was that we had a significant capacity to experience conflict, tension, and stress, and handle it. Not always smoothly, not always without some costs, not always without breaking stride, but we could take a licking and keep on ticking. The congregation seldom polarized around an issue or personal strife. Conflict was handled dynamically, cutting this way one time and that way the next time. Conflicts did not create camps. People could find issues they agreed on and so put their disagreements into perspective. We operated with something I later dubbed parallel tracking: people would opt for new or continuing niches in our multifaceted group life and committee structure which put them into immediate contact with those with whom they could work. Individuals whose approaches did not align gave each other enough berth so that each could contribute his or her gift to the congregation. Thus although we experienced a number of sideswipes, we avoided major head-on collisions, by and large. Yet because we are a small church with a relatively diverse congregation that still prefers whole group events to predominantly subgroup activity, this homogeneity principle had its very real limits in practice. We still had to deal with divergent approaches, but usually in managable doses. And I was surprised at the amount of interpreting and buffeting I was doing.

One illustrative incident occurred relative to our parking problem. This was a good problem to have: not enough space available on summer Sunday mornings. The trustees analyzed the problem from every conceivable perspective. John, a hardnosed, no-nonsense, get-things-done type, wanted to cut down the old hedge behind the church. He would uproot it with his backhoe in an afternoon. Bill, a flowerchild type, thought that such measures were too drastic. Besides, that hedge was the only buffer the church had against the "fragrance" of the neighboring sewer plant. Back and forth the discussion went. Finally, my high-priced negotiating skills could be contained no longer. I proposed we cut down the first half of the hedge. This would give us the majority of the parking and still provide some aromatic buffer. The vote was four to two. Bill and John both voted against my plan, for opposite reasons! I had offered to help with the hedge removal. On the appointed day I showed up with my bow saw, alone. John had decided it wasn't worth getting his backhoe out for just half the hedge, and Bill was last heard mumbling some poem about "Pastor, Pastor, spare that tree!" So I started in on the hedge alone. Well, not quite alone; my dad was visiting

and I had dragged him along to help. But he was no help at all. He
spent the whole afternoon wondering aloud what kind of leader I was.
Couldn't I get anyone to help? His was no word to the wise, as he didn't
seem to consider me in that category, but a whole afternoon lecture! I
used to chuckle over that old story of the man from the Mason-Dixon
Line who couldn't decide whose side to fight on in the Civil War, so he
donned a blue shirt and gray pants and was fired on by both sides! I no
longer consider that story the least bit funny.

The third thing I learned about conflict, stress, and tension in our
congregation was that, not only were we able to handle the stress we
experienced, but we were often able to transform it into energy for
growth in our common life! Just like walking. We utilized the loss of
balance to propel us that next step forward. Not all the time, maybe not
even the majority of times, but often enough that I could see and appreciate the reality of this possibility.

Like the time when our deacon chairman decided to synthesize the
theological and business worlds. He had decided that what we really
need God to forgive us of is our sins, not our debts. (He had, apparently,
just paid off his mortgage!) So he approached me as CEO (as he saw it)
of our congregation to institute this change in our weekly recitation of
the Lord's Prayer in worship. I was pretty sure of two things: we were
not fully ready for such a change, and I did not want to be crucified upon such a cross as that! So I stalled. Old negotiator that he was, he saw
my resistance and raised his insistence. Finally I cried uncle and offered
to bring the matter up for discussion at the church business meeting in a
few weeks. Fine, he said. I duly raised the issue at our meeting after our
other business was concluded. The chairman chimed in with his feelings
and we were off on a lengthy and lively discussion. Actually, it turned
out to be wonderfully productive. It had its points of pathos, as when
one woman told about the spiritual abuse she had endured when she as a
child was forced to dredge up sins to confirm her status as a sinner but
was too young to understand any of it. It had its points of humor, as
when one of our older ladies, having been required by her health to winter in a retirement home in Connecticut, announced that she was for sin
and it was spreading like wildfire throughout the churches of Connecticut. We Rhode Islanders had always suspected so and now we had an
eyewitness! And it had its conclusion in charity, for though the majority
favored the change, all could see that it was a deep and significant issue

for the minority and love deemed us to make no change at this time. I drove home feeling elated. As a congregation we had faced into the wind. We had listened to each other and heard deep feelings being expressed. We had learned a lot and had held ourselves together in love.

I was not able to indulge myself in these feelings for long, though. My mother was visiting and was riding home with me. (There must be something downright Freudian about my parents' presence allowing conflicted energies to surface!) She warned me never to allow such a discussion again. It would split the church! She was reliving a church split she had experienced years before. But her comment underscored for me our congregation's ability to turn stress into growth, to transform crossed energy and align it for progress.

So the invitation of those South Dakota pastors became a great blessing for me. It allowed me to look into stress, to see its presence, to discern the dynamics it triggered, and to start on a road that saw stress as the misaligned energy of personal, pastoral, and congregational growth. This book has grown from the insights I shared in South Dakota.

What Is Pastoral Stress?

Stress may be considered from many different perspectives. Stress may be catalogued relative to its source. Stress may be generated by tensions at work, difficulties in familial relations, existential angst, etc. Stress may also be looked at experientially, as anxiety, generalized or focused, dysfunction, etc. And stress may be considered relative to its result. Thus eustress motivates energy to respond to a challenge; distress is debilitating, a diminishment of constructive response. Already, even in these straightforward categories, you can see overlaps and omissions. So other categories have been posited. One could become stressed simply trying to comprehend stress!

We will make no attempt to be comprehensive in our treatment of stress here. Rather we will focus on stress of a particular type: stress experienced by a pastor in the performance of the pastoral function. And within this focus we will zoom in on a specific definition of stress. Stress will be viewed as the experience of conflicted or crossed energy. The energy of which we speak here is social energy, the energy of persons or groups to continuously bring themselves into being. Thus when the energy of one part of a social reality (in this case, the pastor) crosses with the energy of another part (e.g., specific individuals, the congregation in general, or the social context) to embody their reality, stress results. This stress may be consciously understood, but frequently is not. This stress is experienced by both parties contributing to the crossing, but may not be registered in awareness by both. This book is written to pastors who are registering stress, although congregations and their helpers will benefit by its understandings, too.

Like crossed swords clashing in a duel, stress exists when the expectations of the pastor cross with his or her experience of the surrounding reality. When pastoral hopes are blindsided by congregational happenings, stress results. Although this stress may be generated in many arenas, it is registered in the being of the pastor, heart or mind, psyche or soul. Stress is that internal pain and/or confusion that occurs when energies cross instead of align. If you are a right brain preference person, you may be experiencing a bit of stress as you read sentence after sentence of left brain constructs and definitions. Your expectation to understand in your comfortable patterns is crossing with your experience of the last two paragraphs. I feel stress, too: my expectation of communication may be crossed by your experience of confusion. So let's look at a couple of stress-reducing pictures.

Flying to Block Island: A Parable

I live on Block Island. It is a real island, ten miles out to sea off the southern coast of New England. If one can't walk on water, one gets back or forth by boat or small aircraft. Now Block Island is reputed to be the windiest town in the nation, which means that the ferries do not always run. And when they don't, the small airplanes probably shouldn't either. But they will bravely face up to sixty-mile-an-hour winds to get straying islanders who show up at the airport home again.

This is not always a happy experience. People who are not on speaking terms with the Lord ought not even attempt it. The twelve-minute flight stretches into an eternity as the little plane fights buffeting gusts, malevolent wind shears, and stomach inverting turbulence. And should one desire to come face to face with one's mortality, the process of landing kindly obliges. The island has but one landing strip and it runs east-west. Our gale force winds are typically not influenced by this fact. They usually blow northeast or northwest. This means only one thing: a crosswind landing. Pilots have different strategies to deal with the crosswinds. Some try to sneak up on the runway, travelling into the wind, and then at the last possible second, bank hard on to the end of the runway and set the plane down. Others align with the runway from about a mile out, but in order to stay aligned they must angle the nose of the plane windward, approaching the runway sideways. In either case a last minute gust can make the pilot wrestle with the yoke while we passengers hang on to the bucking bronco of a plane, praying that the wheels will touch ground before the wing tip does. If our prayers go unheeded, we will cartwheel down the runway and, as *Top Gun* puts it, crash and burn.

Passengers, like pilots, have their own means of dealing with crosswinds. On Block Island there is a saying, "There are no atheists in crosswinds." Protestants offer up white-knuckled prayers, silently, with eyes closed and pores open. Catholics keep the blood circulating in their fingers by doing the rosary with such rapidity as to make the Pope proud. Quakers stay true to their appellation! On landing many turn into pantheists, bowing low to Mother Earth in her asphalt incarnation, kissing her repeatedly with great affection and sincerity. What we wouldn't have given for a head wind. But we didn't have that option; it was either stay away from Block Island or land crosswind.

For pastors there is almost always another option. The small aircraft sustains much physical stress as it lands crosswind. So, too, pastors experience much stress as they strive to realize progress in their own direction while enduring forces pushing them off course and endangering their "landing." But pastors can redirect their approach and land into the wind. Facing into the wind is the safe way to land a plane, but facing into the wind is not the way readily chosen by human beings, pastors included. Often, we would rather curse the crosswinds than face into the head winds. In this book, we will not only describe the crosswinds but give handles on facing into the headwinds.

I have been a local church pastor for over eighteen years. But I also minister in other contexts. I write for Christian leaders I may never see. I speak at conferences to people who may never come to Block Island, let alone join our church. And therein lies the crossed energy. I see myself as being able to embrace two forms of ministry: the pastoral ministry on Block Island and the trans-pastoral ministry beyond Block Island. I find these two ministries complementary, energizing, cross-fertilizing, and exciting. But the congregation, in part at least, has a different assessment. A portion feels that I turn my back on them when I embrace this second ministry. An undercurrent of opposition developed. My responses ran a wide gamut: frustration at their opposition to God's will, resentment at their opposition to my will, sadness at their spiritual shortsightedness, irritation at their selfish attitude (We had accepted de-ominational resources when we needed them. Aren't we obligated to share in return?), etc. I found myself white-knuckling it, trying ever harder to land on the runway of my extraparish activities, holding on harder and harder as the crosswinds grew stronger. Crossed energy abounded. I was stressed and there was less energy available in me and in the congregation for positive, constructive ministry.

At this point a wise deacon came by to have a chat with me. Tony, he said, some people are stuck in contrariness. No matter what you, the president, or God does, they'll find something wrong with it. To others you can do no wrong. If you said Jesus was coming tomorrow, they'd rush home and pack their bags. But most of us are in the middle. We try to keep an open mind and an open heart, and we look to you to persuade us about the truth. But you haven't been doing it. We don't know any-thing about what you do off the island. You've been keeping your light under a bushel. I suspect it feels like bragging to you, and you are un-comfortable tooting your own horn. OK, but pitch it a different way. Just let us know what you're up to. You'll be surprised at the support you'll get!

He was right. It was too bad, too, for I had to let go of my victim-ization. Sometimes it feels good feeling bad, when you can blame the other parties. No longer could I blame the opposition for not listening when, in fact, I wasn't speaking. He helped me face into the wind and see another runway, a runway for both pastor and people. A new dimen-sion of ministry opened up. I started sharing not only what I'd been up to but also the basis of my activities: the strength of my congregation! I started inviting key lay people to attend conferences with me, working them into some form of leadership wherever possible. A broader vision started to develop. Oh, there are still naysayers, but now there are also a group of people who affirm these same activities as part of our congrega-tion's ministry.

Stress, then, is an invitation to understanding and undertaking.

Stress is like a metal detector with a harsh-sounding buzzer. We may not like to experience it, but it almost always indicates something below the surface that bears greater exploration. The task of realigning crossed energy into coordinated energy is a ministry task, a pastoral undertaking. Stress allows this agenda to surface and thus can be the occasion for congregational transformation.

The Five Arenas of Pastoral Stress

We will consider five arenas of stress. I chose the word arena rather than dimension or aspect because arena conveys the sense of place, of location, a context. Stress is viewed as operating in five distinguishable places in the life of a pastor. These five places overlap and interact. They are not finally discreet, separable, either/or phenomena. The pastor's life is like a five-ring circus or a five-arena rodeo. These arenas are the intrapersonal, the interpersonal, the pastoral role image, the congregational, and the environmental. Crossed energy can be present in any of these arenas, but it may take different forms. Stress in the environmental arena may be felt as more globalized, hard to sink one's teeth into, whereas stress in the congregational arena may be felt as personal animosity. The intrapersonal arena differs somewhat from the other four in that it is both a "source" of stress and the place where stress is registered. Congregations, for example, can be experiencing major amounts of crossed energy, even to the point of trauma, but it is not pastoral stress until the pastor registers it internally. We will look at multiple handles on understanding stress and responding to it for each arena.

Let us briefly note the parameters of each arena.

● **Intrapersonal.** The intrapersonal arena concerns the inner life of the pastor. We will argue that the psyche and the soul ought not to be differentiated too sharply if stress is to be registered and transformed. Soulstress, as I call it, can become a great asset to the pastor who develops the ability to turn six breakdowns into breakthroughs.

● **Interpersonal.** The interpersonal refers to the stress generated in the relationship between the pastor and other individuals related to the congregation. Four aspects of this arena will be considered: personal styles, psychological temperaments, Transactional Analysis, and levels of interpersonal breakdown, from offense to pathology.

● **Pastoral Role Stress.** This arena focuses on the crossed energy
resulting from differences between the pastor and the congregation in
understanding and expectations of what it means to be pastor. Differences over the tasks of the pastor, the essential pastoral function, and the
symbolic meaning behind pastoral roles are seen as generating pastoral
role stress.

● **Congregational Stress.** This arena considers stress that is generated in the functioning of the congregation. Crossed energy can occur in
the patterns of communication and power, in family systems dynamics,
in congregational paradigms differing with size, and in misunderstand-
ings of the congregation's culture and life-cycle position.

● **Environmental stress.** This arena considers stress generated by
dynamics occurring in the social environment around the church and by
the church's attempt to relate to that environment. Often the church is
discussed as if it were a self-contained entity. But the social environment in which the church is located has an enormous capacity to affect
the church. When these influences are not understood and registered,
stress results. Crossed energy can result from different thinking across
generations, different "cultural" orientations, different orientations to
life, different congregational postures, and different understandings of
the church's position in society.

Within each arena, and for most subtopics, the following format will
be used: Forces, Sources, Recourses, and Resources. Forces will explore the dynamics at work, the nature of the energy that can get crossed.
Sources will point out the particular ways in which stress is experienced.
Recourses will offer alternative strategies for transforming stress into
growth. Resources will cite materials for a deeper treatment of the
subject.

Three Stress-Transforming Tools

Three benefits will result from reading this book. 1) **Framing.** This book will provide a useful frame of reference to someone seeking an understanding of stress, the work of the pastor, and congregational life. 2) **Naming.** Pastors (and/or congregations) who feel trapped in stressful situations will be able to name the forces with which they have been wrestling. Even if they choose to regard their particular "crossed energy" as their "cross to bear" in ministering in their congregation, that insight alone can be stress transforming. 3) **Taming.** Taming a wild beast puts its strength and energy at your disposal. So, too, with stress, crossed energy. Means of transforming nonproductive or destructive energy into energy for growth and edification will be shared. The result will be a capacity to shape a deeper pastoral agenda.

A Theological, Hopeful Word

To paraphrase a kindergarten teacher I once had, "Stress is my friend." I don't always believe that myself, but I am getting there. Stress can be my friend, if I see it as a nudge from God. Stress can be an angel, a messenger from God. Stress can be the pinch that wakes you up, the call that alerts you to something worth knowing, the push that gets you started in God's direction. Stress can be all of those things and more. But, of course, we have to believe that stress which feels so painful can be transformed into a necessary ingredient for growth. We have to believe that crossed energies are still energies, dynamic, powerful, and energizing. And that they can be aligned and made productive. We have to believe that stress is our friend, a form of God's healing, redeeming, nurturing presence in our lives. If we do, then "all things are possible to [those] who believe."

CHAPTER 2

Soul Stress – Turning Intrapersonal Breakdowns into Breakthroughs

The Forces at Work

Stress may be triggered by numerous and sundry external events, but it is registered as stress internally, in the heart of the pastor. This intrapersonal stress, or soul stress, is actually an Early Warning System, an invaluable indicator to the pastor. Let us explore the experience of stress, how it is registered, and how it may be transformed. We will consider a number of perspectives, all contributing to our understanding that the soul of the pastor is a powerful, God-given resource to be valued and utilized in registering and tranforming stress.

Theological

One Sunday while on sabbatical, I visited a church where for thirty-five minutes I was berated for being a hapless and virtually hopeless sinner, with whom God would never converse, and then for three minutes told that (but not how) Christ could yet, maybe, speak a saving word to me. I'm not going back there, but it did cause me to wonder. If a person were to hear this message once, twice, or even three times a week, fifty-two weeks a year for, oh, twenty years or so, what effect would it have on his or her self-image and self-understanding? And if this position were reinforced with hymns proclaiming the person's wretchedness and worminess, he might (I did, actually) come to believe that he is only able to hear God's voice in one form: thundering down in judgement.

    The Bible deals clearly with sin (and does not fall into the sin of being so fascinated with it as to move it into the position of a primary reality of God's created order). But it also gives us some clear insight into God's valuation of the human soul.

*In Genesis 1, we read, "Then God said, 'Let us make humankind in our image, in our likeness' . . . So God created humankind in the divine image...and God blessed them."

*In Psalm 139, it clearly says, "For you (God) created my inmost being; I praise you because I am fearfully and wonderfully made; your works are wonderful, I know that full well."

*And in Philippians it states, "It is God who works in you."

So God made us, God made us like divinity itself, and God made us in such a way that we are the locus of God's activity. When God speaks, we can listen! We have the God-given capacity to register God's deeds and words, God's truth, and we do this in our very being. This truth is nothing new. Old Testament characters heard the voice of Lord all the time. And in the New Testament, Jesus and Paul and Peter and John and others got direct messages from the Eternal One. It is inherent in the Protestant doctrine of the priesthood of all believers that full communion with God is available to each and every Christian. That we have, in practice, reduced this doctrine to mean that God is obliged to listen when we decide to speak, and have forgotten our individual ability to listen when God speaks, is truly our loss. Christian prophets and mystics down through the centuries have heard "the word of the Lord." Today our emphasis on the objective word (the Bible) has displaced the subjective words of God (hearing God's word in our soul) not to second place, but to no place at all.[1] "Speak, Lord, for your servant is listening." (I Samuel 3:9f) Samuel believed that if he listened he would be able to hear the words of God. "I am about to do something that will make the ears of everyone who hears of it tingle!" said the Lord. Maybe our spiritual ears do not tingle because, unlike Samuel, we don't believe that we can hear the Lord speaking to us. Or we don't know how to listen.

Psychological

In our society a major distinction is made between the spiritual and the psychological. This disjuncture is reinforced by the psychological professions that do not want to be tied to religion. But it is also fed by our pseudosophistication that has displaced God from every realm of reality that is distinguishable and installed God as sovereign of the "soul," an entity of such ambiguity that it might as well mean "Whatever isn't claimed by anyone else." This is unfortunate. The Greeks had a better word for it. *Psyche* was one reality in Greek thought, not two as in English, the object of religion and psychology. Originally, then, God was to be found "at work" in *psyche*-ological processes, for the soul was the domain of the self and the vessel of God's presence. Carl Jung helps us reunite the two meanings of *psyche*. He regards the deeper levels of the psyche as God's chief means of communication with us! Jung writes:

> Christians often ask why God does not speak to them, as he is believed to have done in former days. When I hear such questions, it always makes me think of the rabbi who was asked how it could be that God often showed himself to people in the olden days while nowadays nobody sees him. The rabbi replied: "Nowadays there is no longer anybody who can bow low enough." This answer hits the nail on the head. We are so captivated by and entangled in our . . . consciousness that we have forgotten the age-old fact that God speaks chiefly through dreams and visions . . . the Christian puts his Church and his Bible between himself and his unconscious.[2]

As will be shown later, I would like to add other psychological processes to the means of God's speaking to us. But Jung clearly points us to the truth that by listening to what is going on within our psyches we can hear God.

Mythological

Many peoples have stories that point out the internal connection between humans and the divine. As I am studying the Hopis (a Native American tribe of about 10,000, located in northern Arizona, with much of their culture relatively intact) at this time, let me share their picture of "open door" communication possible between individual humans and the Creator.

For seven or eight years he (the Hopi child) led the normal earthly life of a child. Then came his first initiation into a religious society, and he began to learn that, although he had human parents, his real parents were the universal entities who had created him through them—his Mother Earth, from whose flesh all are born, and his Father Sun, the solar god who gives life to all the universe. He began to learn, in brief, that he too had two aspects. He was a member of an earthly family and tribal clan, and he was a citizen of the great universe, to which he owed a growing allegiance as his understanding developed.

The First People, then, understood the mystery of their parenthood. In their pristine wisdom they also understood their own structure and functions—the nature of man himself.

The living body of man and the living body of the earth were constructed in the same way. Through each ran an axis, man's axis being the backbone, the vertebral column, which controlled the equilibrium of his movements and his functions. Along this axis were several vibratory centers that echoed the primordial sound of life throughout the universe or sounded a warning if anything went wrong.

The first of these centers in man lay at the top of the head. Here, when he was born, was the soft spot, *kopavi,* the "open door" through which he received his life and communicated with his Creator. For with every breath the soft spot moved up and down with a gentle vibration that was communicated to the Creator.[3]

I received another story from a Native American source.

There is a legend that tells how the Ancient Ones determined where to hide the power of the universe, so that man would not find and abuse it. One thought the safest place to hide it would be on top of the highest mountain. Another suggested hiding it at the bottom of the sea. A third recommended that the power be hidden in the central core of the earth. One by one, the locations were rejected: the Ancients knew that man would go to any height, depth, or distance to obtain the sacred power. In the end, they decided to hide the power of the universe within man himself, reasoning that he would never think to look there. And that is where it remains hidden to this very day.[4]

The power of the universe transcends slightly what I am trying to point to, but the power to function better in your universe, your psychological, interpersonal, and congregational universe is, indeed, hidden within you.

Physiological

Recent studies reveal an interesting fact about gender differences in the human brain. The right hemisphere is the center of more wholistic, pictorial, gestalt thinking. The left hemisphere is the center of more analytical, linear, "logical" thought. Researchers have recently noted that the cord or "cable" that connects the two hemispheres tends to be thicker in women than in men. More activity or inter-hemisphere talk can occur in women than in men. Is this the source of "women's intuition"? Some say yes. Women are able to process a wider range of clues in any given situation, and sometimes come away with intuitive conclusions that cannot be defended with left brain logic. Interestingly, men register the same clues, but their cable cannot bear the traffic to process them as thoroughly. In other words, often the information we need to move to a deeper level of understanding is already within us if we could but avail ourselves of it. This is more than a matter of men catching up to women. All of us could do better thinking if we could develop our intuitive or integrated thought processes.

The Internal Dynamism

We can sum up the theological, psychological, mythological, and physiological perspectives by saying: You are your own best resource! You are your own best resource for transforming stress into positive, spiritual, pastoral progress. (This is not to discount the work of the Holy Spirit, but to acknowledge it and release it to greater levels of effectiveness.) Your being, your psyche, your soul is designed by God to register more reality than your "head" can recognize and process. Frequently, what is picked up are things that are out of alignment, mismatched or crossed: stress. Soulstress is one of God's ways of talking to you. Soulstress is your soul registering things that are crossed, or in conflict, in your world.

Soulstress is the evidence that expectations and experiences are in tension. Soulstress is the message that encodes a spiritual/pastoral agenda.

Soulstress is a gift from God that we usually send back unopened, even unacknowledged because soulstress is often painful and always requires work. We like things to be happy and harmonious. When pain comes we seek to insulate ourselves, anesthetize ourselves, or run away from it. To look into the pain and explore it is to increase the pain, at least in the short term. But by training ourselves, with God's help, to learn from the pain and grow from it, we can turn the stress to our profit. This process requires effort. But it is effort that results in our increasing spiritual maturity and more effective pastoring. In other words, it is effort that is worth the effort!

Initial recognition of soulstress occurs through internal pain or confusion. Pain we experience as anxiety, shame, worry, lament, anger, etc. If it helps, we might call this aspect of soulstress heartache, and the next headache, as long as we can keep in mind that these are two sides of one coin: soulstress. Headache we experience as confusion, craziness, illogicality, unreasonableness, stubbornness, stupidity, etc. We might say that soulstress has both emotional and cognitive triggers, as long as we remember that these two aspects overlap and intertwine. There are at least six sources of soulstress that I have been able to identify in my pastoring. Maybe you will be able to add some more from your experience. I will be gratified if I can communicate an approach that is helpful to you in doing this. Remember, YOU are your own best resource: God talks to you in your stress. God seeks to use your stress to help you mature as a person and to help you gain effectiveness as a pastor. In the face of stress, you are your own best resource to effect God's purpose.

Sources of Stress

The six sources of soulstress are dissonance, deviation, resistance, transference, anxiety, and dreams. Typically, we experience these dynamics as stress, cognitive and emotional, as breakdowns in the life of the congregation which are registering in our souls, as landmines along the pastoral road we have chosen to walk. We feel them as pain or as confusion, as intrusions or obstacles to true ministry. Instead of trying to rush past them (I'm not sure that is actually possible, but we tend to keep trying!), let us pause to name them and thus start the process of exploring them.

1. **Dissonance**. Dissonance is a fancy word that means "That doesn't make any sense!" Most healthy people and congregations behave in reasonably functional, logical, and constructive ways. If your church is plunking along and, all of a sudden, people, boards, committees, or subgroups start acting irrationally, temporary insanity need not be the reason. This dissonant behavior may be your clue to deeper dynamics you have yet to realize. Sarah had adjusted to life without children. It was disappointing, but that was reality. At her age hers was the logical, reasonable posture: accept childlessness. So when that strange fellow came along and announced her due date, she sniggered and said, under her breath, "This guy's crazy!" But the situation was more pregnant than she thought. In Isaac she learned a great lesson and received a great blessing. Unfortunately for us, God's truths do not often come to our consciousness if we ignore or discount them. We have to register and nurture God's clues.

2. **Resistance**. Resistance is just what it implies, psychological or administrative foot-dragging in the presence of what is touted as a great step forward. I often find myself resisting things that are new (and therefore anxiety producing), things that imply my performance to date was inadequate in some way, great ideas that someone else thought of, etc. But, of course, the congregation is much better at resistance than I ever thought of being. (Maybe they have to be to protect themselves from me!) Resistance can be active or passive, obvious or subtle, but it always feels frustrating to the proposer of "the great idea." Yet resistance can play a positive role in the congregation's life. First of all, some great ideas aren't actually so great and should be resisted. Resistance, in this case, is the polite form of "You idiot. That is a stupid idea." And given my frequency of such ideas, I'm all for courtesy. But more important, when the proposal is a valid one, resistance indicates that the time is not ripe. Resistance is not necessarily a sign of evil. It may mean that more explanation, exposure, or understanding is indicated. Or, and this is frequently the case, it may mean that the issues involved are much deeper than originally thought. In other words, it is a call to ministry.

Jonah engaged in resistance. God called him to get going and he did—but in the opposite direction! Fortunately for Nineveh and Jonah,

God considered Jonah's resistance a sign for the need of growth. God hung with him. We find that the resistance masked Jonah's conflictedness and his indulgence. Jonah was conflicted regarding his greatest hope and his worst fear. His greatest hope was that God was a merciful and forgiving God. His greatest fear was that God was a merciful and forgiving God. He wanted to claim God's forgiveness for himself, while denying it to the Ninevehites. And so he wanted to indulge his desire for revenge. It is interesting to me that the Book of Jonah does not end with the salvation of Nineveh, but with God still dealing with Jonah's resistance, offering Jonah another chance to overcome his spiritual myopia!

3. **Transference**. Transference is the process of releasing emotional energy not in the situation that has generated it but in a safer, closer, or more secure situation. We have all had the experience of making an innocuous or minor remark and receiving a reaction of Vesuvian magnitude. Transference is occuring when we are left in the dust with our mouths hanging open and our minds utterly confounded. A typical response is to protect oneself from such incidents in the future or roundly blame the volcanic impersonator. (Of course, we never act like that!) A more helpful response is to attempt to track down the origin of the extra energy. Transference poses quite a challenge because of the dearth of clues left at the scene of the eruption. Sometimes you can review recent events in that person's life for insight. Sometimes friends will have a clue about what's eating Vesuvius. Sometimes both of you coming clean will work. Sometimes prayer and patience.

Let me clarify that transference does not always lead to a "blow out." That is its most clear instance. But any occasion when emotional energy is applied to an "innocent" bystander is transference. The game Joseph played with his brothers when they came to Egypt to buy grain is transference. From the emotions he later displayed it is obvious that Joseph brought much emotional energy to the events following his recognition of his brothers. But he didn't display them initially. They found their outlet in the game that he was playing with them—a game that they did not "get." Confusion and anxiety were their response, along with the required inability to please the transferer. If the brothers had been more astute they might have figured out the reason behind Joseph's transference. Fortunately, he "fessed up" in time for a loving reunion. O, that there would always be such an outcome in our churches!!

An example. I had been wrestling with three problems in my congregation. How to assure a quorum at Board meetings in the face of
declining attendance. How to increase our Friends' (a type of affiliation
for seasonal people) awareness and involvement in the workings of our
church. How to tap into more energy to help with our summer ministries. The idea to elect a Friend to each main board of the church presented itself. It was a partial, but helpful, solution. All fall I pitched the
idea to the church leaders. It met with nodded heads. (A sure indicator
of nothing in particular, I was about to discover!) In January, I raised it
at our congregation's annual meeting, trusting in its obvious logic and its
small scale impact to assure its passage. In fact, I thought most people
would sleep through the discussion of its merits. But what happened
woke me up! The motion was read and explained. I chimed in with its
benefits. A long and spirited but confusing discussion followed. Despite
the amount of time spent on the discussion no consensus or even clarity
was reached. In fact, the motion had to be repeatedly explained in the
face of recurring misinterpretations of its implications. People were
acting as if this motion was intricate and convoluted, when in fact the
motion itself was simple and straight forward. The response was
"crazy." Dissonance had struck.

At one point a Deacon, frustrated with the discussion, commented
that moving to bolster the chances for quorum at our board meetings
would not be necessary if the board members (= church members) were
more committed. His comment was interpreted as challenging the commitment of the Friends, and it triggered another round of comments regarding the low commitment level of the Friends. The misinterpretation,
the thinly veiled accusations, and the length of time being consumed with
no forward progress whatsoever, indicated to me that a major portion of
the congregation had gone into Resistance. There was more here than
met the ear, but I had no idea what it was. When the moderator suggested calling the question, I asked that it be sent back to the Executive
Board for more consideration instead. Well, that motion passed!

As the more perfunctory portions of the meeting transpired, I went
into deep consideration. I had been surprised twice that night. Once
when the topic of my proposed sabbatical came up. It engendered almost
no discussion whatsoever, a couple of positive comments and well
wishes from the moderator and on to the next item of the agenda. I had
expected and was prepared for mixed feelings and reactions, but virtual

silence had caught me by surprise. And second when the Friends-on-Board had been verbosely confounded back to committee. Ah, of course. Transference was at work! The mixed feelings regarding my sabbatical plans, if expressed, might be construed as an attack on Tony whom we like and don't want to attack. But on the other hand, he is proposing to leave us for three months and that makes us feel like attacking something! Ah, yes, Tony's pet idea about these Friends is just the thing!

Ah, but the onion has even more layers. At our men's group a couple weeks later, the "craziness" of the Friends discussion came up. One of the men mentioned that it didn't seem quite so crazy to him. Do you remember when summer residents would complain about the way the town was run, and our answer was, Well, if you care so much why don't you register to vote here? And then they did! And now at town meetings the year round residents are frequently outvoted by seasonal people! While we recognize the legality of it all, it leaves us with the feeling of not being in control of our own town, of our own destiny. Well, it's kind of the same with Friends. Church members feel that these summer people are less committed to the church and that the church members will end up on the outside looking in if Friends are given too much say. Logically, one Friend could do no such thing, but the feeling of being undermined and victimized made me pause. Friends were friends to me and the source of a number of new members. In addition, as an individual I feel a sense of potency in the congregation and in the community, but obviously (now) not all members feel that way. The dissonance and resistance had revealed an attitude of impotency in the congregation that I had not registered previously. What to do about it? I don't know yet, but an area of ministry has been clarified to me.

As this example illustrates, "clues" can come in bunches and point to multiple solutions. The world isn't simple enough to allow us the luxury of dealing with one thing at a time and having that one thing always have a unitary solution. Life is dynamic and that is what makes "intuiting" fun!

4. **Deviation**. Deviation refers to a change from the normal, an event out of the ordinary, unexpected, unpredicted. Obvious examples in church life are increases or decreases in attendance or offering. These red flags point to a change of heart or circumstance. But any change in the behavior of the congregation as a whole or in individual members is a clue

waiting to be read. Moses noted a deviation. All the bushes he had seen burning during his lifetime had burned up. But that one particular day he saw a burning bush that was not being burned up. Did Moses say, "You can't depend on anything, nowadays"? No. He said, "Well, that's different. I'd better check it out." Moses ended up on holy ground. We may not, but we will at least learn something of significance.

5. **Anxiety**. Anxiety grows out of a perceived threat to our expectations or desires. Anxiety can be in me, in the other, in the group or system or in any combination. Anxiety can be trivial or world threatening. But anxiety always points to something of spiritual significance. Anxiety is an internal warning system pointing out a perceived danger to something we value. Thus the presence of anxiety allows us the opportunity to look at what we consider a danger and at what we consider valuable. If you feel anxious upon entering a group for the first time, your anxiety might be asking you "What is the source of your self-confidence, what is the basis of your self-image?" If interpersonal relations habitually trigger anxieties in you, your anxiety might be directing you to reassess the functionality of your emotional system. Maybe you feel as if your core world is threatened. Harry Emerson Fosdick described religious traditions as the "home of the soul." Your anxiety is inviting you to look afresh at your spiritual home. Is it built upon a solid foundation? Is there room to be alone, room to be together, room to grow? If you are the one feeling the anxiety, can you learn from it? If a loved one or the congregation is feeling anxious, can you be a "nonanxious presence" helping them to work through their anxiety to wrest the spiritual blessing that God has hidden in it? Owen Owens makes a telling point in an environmental manuscript. He says that Miles Standish, feeling threatened by the Native Americans, went out to fight them with muskets, after refusing to pray. Owens wonders had Standish been able to bring his anxieties to God in prayer if the whole course of English-Indian history might not have been different![5]

6. **Dreams**. Although the Bible is full of God speaking in dreams, most post-Jungians would say our dreams are simply a more basic part of ourselves talking. Yet it seems to me that God can speak through basic or sophisticated parts of the human mind. Maybe even better through the basic. For me, dreams name what my conscious mind does not want to deal with. Fears about the future, unresolved issues, broken relation-

ships, ignored potentials. My dreams do not provide me with answers, but they clue me into some of the right questions.

A recent experience in my family caught me up short, even scared me. It is anecdotal to be sure but, I think, illustrative of the dream manifestation of soulstress. It goes like this:

In the sixteenth year of my pastoring on Block Island, I brought up the possibility of a sabbatical. In addition to the regular business of the Deacons, Executive Board, and congregational meetings during my seventeenth year, a plan for my sabbatical was mutually formulated and approved. The responses of the members of the congregation ranged from exceedingly enthusiastic to exceedingly hesitant. (The former concerned me almost as much as the latter!) Some perceived it as an extended vacation and most of these felt I deserved it and needed it. Some, mostly those with academic or corporate backgrounds, grasped the idea and supported it. Some saw it only as an absence: our pastor will be away all winter. Among the latter group was a matriarch of the church. She is a dedicated Christian woman with whom I have a very positive relationship, most of the time. But on two separate occasions as the day drew nigh for my departure, she articulated her anxiety. Only once previously had she really needed a pastor. (She is over fifty years old so this alone was a humbling thought!!) That was when her teenage son was in the throes of a full scale adolescent rebellion, threatening to run away and marry a woman whom everyone except the starstruck kid could see was totally inappropriate. She needed spiritual counsel, encouragement, and perspective but she couldn't turn to her pastor because he had been struck by a hit and run driver and had spent most of that year in the hospital. She fully recognized that it was not his fault, but she still felt his absence. Not to worry, I assured her. Bad things don't always happen. And besides we've arranged for a very fine interim pastor. Lay people were handling things for three weeks and then the interim would arrive.

As fate (?!) would have it, my family and I had no sooner arrived in Arizona on my sabbatical when we received the bad news. Her husband had suffered a heart attack, had almost died, and was now awaiting surgery! We called, we prayed, we wrote, we worried. My anxiety was pushing my limits. I was concerned that the husband pull through (he did). I was concerned about the wife receiving the support she needed (she seems to have). And I was worried about my own "failure" to be present. As the drama played out for over two weeks, I tried very hard

to keep my anxiety in control and not ruin my family's daily life. With
private praying and sharing with my wife, I thought I was doing OK.

Then one morning at breakfast my twelve-year-old daughter announced that she had had a strange dream. Oh? What was that, dear?
Well, [matriarch] was making a bed in the church, when the church
caught on fire. People called and called to her, but she wouldn't come
out. Why? It was her job to make the bed and she was going to make
the bed, no matter what. How did the dream end? I dunno. The church
was still burning and she was still making the bed when I woke up.

Somehow my daughter's unconscious had registered both the matriarch's anxiety and my anxiety!! She had processed it in a way that I
could read. The matriarch's spiritual structure was in danger. *She* was
sticking with the church (whatever the pastor did)! She was making her
bed in the house of the Lord. But the dream hadn't come to an end. The
outcome was still open.

Her dream was a further invitation to me to face into the pain of not
being able to be Superpastor, all things to all people, every time! To
trust God to put out the flames of destruction, and to accept that there are
circumstances in which one can take a respite from duty, pastoring or
bed making! About two days later I was awakened by a phone call from
Block Island (Arizona is two hours behind). "We're home," the matriarch bubbled. "He's weak but fine. Love you and miss you. See you for
Easter."

Recourses for Transformation

There are three strategies for responding to soulstress in a transformational way. They represent three ways to look into soulstress pain and
confusion and work to learn its lessons. For ease in remembering I have
labelled these three recourses as prayer, share, and care.

Let us first consider the overall strategy. Its first element is to look
into the pain, to live in its presence, and by doing so, begin to see it for
what it is. Our usual approach to pain is to do anything, anything, but
to face into it. We turn away from it, we deny it, we let it buffet us into
all kinds of dysfunctional behaviors, we act out, we project. We would
rather do anything than face into the pain. But as Jesus "set his face
toward Jerusalem" and "endured the cross," so too we must set our face

into the pain and experience it, if we desire spiritual life and growth, and if we desire to be pastors responsive to God's leading.

I once read of a rancher who purchased a herd composed of two breeds of cattle. In fine weather both breeds did well. But when winter's first blizzard struck, the cattle of one breed, seeking to escape the harshness of the wind, turned away and were driven by the wind into gulleys, ravines, and snowdrifts where many died. The other breed turned to face into the wind, stood next to each other and held their ground. They all survived.[6]

We must face into the wind and look into the pain. As necessary as it is to "face" and "look," these words are too passive to convey the active and even aggressive posture necessary to turn soulstress into spiritual fodder. "Work"[7] and "wrestle" are better words. In Genesis 32 we are given a wonderful story about wresting a blessing. Jacob was preparing to reenter Palestine after an absence of some twenty years and meet his brother Esau whom he had tricked out of his inheritance. Jacob was so distraught over this upcoming encounter that he connived a number of ploys to "buy off" Esau. (What Jacob does not and cannot know at his level of spiritual maturity is that Esau has had a spiritual transformation and is ready to meet Jacob in a spirit of joy, love, and reconciliation. But Jacob can only project his own feelings—revenge—and enact his own solution—bargaining—onto the situation.) His anxiety is so great that he cannot sleep during the night before the encounter. Instead he wrestles all night with an unidentified man/god/spirit. My interpretation is that he is wrestling with the personification of his own anxiety sent by God to teach him a spiritual lesson. As daybreak approached, the wrestler prepares to leave. (This wrestler is not a thing existing in the light of day, but a dynamic within Jacob's own soul, which at this point is still pretty dark!) But, interestingly enough, Jacob has wrestled with this spirit all night and wrestled well. (I wrestled in high school and I know how much effort is expended in just three two-minute rounds. Wrestling all night involves a phenomenal amount of work.) He has wrestled all night and has gained a slight advantage over the spirit. So Jacob intends to cash in! He asks for the spirit's name. In Biblical thought one's name is more than a label; it involves personal power and essential identity. To name is to have power over and to shape or reveal identity.[8] Jacob wants a handle on this spirit for future advantage. Instead the spirit gives Jacob a handle on himself! The spirit renames

Jacob! It gives him a wonderful name: God-striver! But what does that mean? One who strives for God? Or with God? Either way Jacob is given the insight that he exists to battle on the spiritual plane! It seems that it will be many more years before he enacts this new identity, but, undoubtedly, the fruit of this all night wrestling match—a new name/identity—brings energy to that process.

Transforming soulstress into spiritual growth and insight demands work. But God is ready and willing to bless us in our wrestling! Let us now consider the three contexts of this wrestling.

Prayer

By prayer I do not mean a casual request for God's presence. I do not mean unilateral instructions directed toward the divine. I do not mean a plea for relief. I mean rather a sincere opening of the heart and mind to the message God has placed within the soulstress. This prayer requires the belief that there is a blessing in the pain and confusion. That from the pain may come an impetus to change and from the confusion may come an insight into deeper truth. It is an examination of the stress. An asking of why does this hurt. What is it within me that experiences this situation in this way? (Situations do not specify how they are to be experienced. We color situations from our own soul. Jacob experienced Esau's approach as heavy duty anxiety. In reality, joy would have been the appropriate response. His anxiety was a mirror on his soul. It was not situationally caused.) What energy am I crossing with the energy of the situation?

Some people enact this kind of prayer in meditation. Some will go on a retreat to a center or a mini-retreat at a quiet place close to home. They will designate a block of time as "wrestling time." I, on the other hand, am a muller. And I am not terribly courageous. I approach the pain and when it starts to hurt too much, I back off and circle around and come at it again from a little different angle. Sometimes I think I exhaust the soulstress until it just gives up and yields its message to me. Other times I exhaust myself and do not reap its blessing. Slowly I am learning that soulstress is my friend, a form of God talking to me. Slowly I am learning to dare to listen more.

Share

If we already knew the message within the stress, it would not come to us as stress but as task, duty, or agenda. It is because it is, at least to some degree, hidden from us that we experience it as soulstress. And oftentimes the more we try to see what is invisible to us, the further it recedes. My daughter came home from school one day to share the funny incident of the confused teacher. Seems a young upstart had taped an unpleasant meassge on the teacher's back. Each time he turned his back on a new portion of the class, giggles erupted. The more he turned to locate the cause of this unscholarly behavior, the worse the behavior became. Needless to say little was learned that day!

Sometimes we just can't see what is invisible to us no matter how hard we try.[9] We need the help of others. John writes that fellowship with God through Jesus Christ is not enough. Fellowship with one another is also needed. (I John 1:2-4) This fellowship for the purpose of exploring soulstress may be found with spouse, friends, and/or collegial groups. My insular life makes meeting with other clergy difficult. Fortunately, my wife and certain key friends in the congregation and community help me in the process of transforming soulstress into spiritual growth. I am repeatedly saddened by clergy who live in the proximity of congenial clergy but who do not avail themselves of the resource of one another. Inertia, laziness, competitiveness, fear of intimacy, fear of dependency? I do not know what is holding us back, but if we intend to grow in God's will, we need to help one another.[10]

Care

Sometimes the soulstress is of such a degree that professional care is indicated. Dream work is especially difficult for an untrained person. Sometimes anxiety or one's own resistance or transference can become dysfunctional. Finding trained help is a means of staying on the "Jesus way." People who think it's "hip" to have their own therapist and those who would never consider professional care, both puzzle me. It seems to me that the wise person reaches out and obtains the necessary resources for health and coping with soulstress as necessary. On three occasions in my life I have availed myself of professional help. One was in the

middle of a year-long bout with Lyme disease. I was making some physical progress, but all of a sudden I lost interest in church life, food, the
Red Sox, and murder mysteries! Something very serious was going on,
but what? Life hardly seemed worth the effort; I could barely drag myself out of bed in the morning. When it became clear that this was not
getting better on its own, I set up an appointment with a pastoral counsellor. After hearing me out and asking a lot of questions, he announced
that I had a classical case of depression. Boy, was I elated to find out
that all I had was depression! Just naming it helped me turn the corner
in dealing with it. Most denominations have made a solid effort to make
trained helpers available to their clergy. I hope we can find a way to
make this resource more integral in pastoral life.

Conclusion

You are your own best resource. Trust yourself—your feelings, your intuition, your stress, your God. Learn to read yourself—what you are registering, feeling and experiencing—and you will receive God's message.

Resources for Further Study

Baylor, Byrd and Peter Parnall, *The Other Way to Listen,* New York:
Charles Scribners' Sons, 1978.

Dooling, D.M. and Paul Jordan-Smith, eds., *I Become Part of It: Sacred
Dimension in Native American Life,* New York: Parabola Books, 1989.

Hands, Donald R. and Wayne L. Fehr, *Spiritual Wholeness for Clergy:
A New Psychology of Intimacy with God, Self, and Others,* Washington,
DC: The Alban Institute, 1993.

Harbaugh, Gary L., *Caring for the Caregiver: Growth Models for
Professional Leaders and Congregations,* Washington, DC: The Alban
Institute, 1992.

Harris, John C., *Stress, Power, and Ministry,* Washington, DC: The Alban Institute, 1977.

Johnson, Robert A., *Inner Work Using Dreams and Active Imagination for Personal Growth,* San Francisco: Harper and Row, 1986.

McRae-McMahon, Dorothy, *Being Clergy, Staying Human: Taking Our Stand in the River,* Washington, DC: The Alban Institute, 1992.

Oswald, Roy M., *Clergy Self-Care: Finding a Balance for Effective Ministry,* Washington, DC: The Alban Institute, 1991.

Oswald, Roy M., *How to Build a Support System for Your Ministry,* Washington, DC: The Alban Institute, 1991.

Peck, M. Scott, *The Road Less Travelled: A New Psychology of Love, Traditional Values and Spiritual Growth,* New York: Simon & Schuster, 1978.

CHAPTER 3

Interpersonal Stress

Introduction

Interpersonal stress is, obviously, the stress experienced when energy crosses in the relationship between two persons. Some experience more stress than others; some handle it better than others. But no one is immune from interpersonal stress. One could argue that this is a dynamic necessary to being human. Everyone experiences interpersonal stress.

But there are some ways in which pastors are in a position to receive more than their "fair share." For example, the guts of pastoring is interpersonal relationships. For an assembly line worker or a stock market analyst, relating to people is but a fraction of their vocational duties. Not so for the pastor; it *is* his or her vocational duty! No wonder Jesus got up early and went off to pray in the wilderness, leaving his disciples to wonder where he was. Second, as a representative of Christ, of love incarnated in human form, pastors often place upon themselves the obligations to make each of these relationships sweet and harmonious. This is a cultural definition of love, not Christ's, and a sure prescription for stress.

Pastors can run, but they can't hide from interpersonal stress. And they can't run very far either.

Pastors, as well as the rest of humanity, typically deal with interpersonal stress with a combination of unproductive strategies including extra-location, globalization, and immutability. Extra-location is a fancy way of saying, "It's not my fault; it's the other person's." There is often enough truth in this claim to prevent a fearless and searching analysis of what is happening. This leads to immutability. Because it is the other person's fault and no one can ultimately control anyone else, well, we're just stuck with a stressful relationship. The self-illusory dream of the other person fixing the problem masks the fixedness we have created in that interpersonal stress. It is immutable. Or it is globalized. "We just don't get along." "I can't stand him and the feeling is mutual." "We're so different." Etc. The function of globalization is the same as extra-location and immutability: it allows us to feel self-righteous in the midst of a stressful interpersonal relationship by pretending a resolution or at least progress toward one is not possible.

But if we were to scratch most instances of interpersonal stress I believe we would find that there is a pattern to our stress. In fact, I think that we would find that most of our interpersonal stress falls into one (or more) of five relational dynamics. We can label these as stylistic, temperamental, transactional, offensive/pathological, and motivational. We will consider the first four in this chapter and the fifth in the next chapter because of its implications regarding the pastoral role in addition to the pastor as person.

Stylistic Differences

Forces at Work and Sources of Stress

The Rev. Cabriolet Nash loved her parish. It was located in a stable urban neighborhood with people of varied backgrounds. Serving for not quite a year yet, the honeymoon glow was still in evidence. She loved her people. So why did she hate coffee hour so much? It should be the best hour of the week, chatting about worship, catching up on each other's lives, making connections for the week ahead. But instead she dreaded it. This week she was determined she would find out why.

The last hand shaken, Cabriolet took a deep breath and headed for Fellowship Hall. Already her anxiety was mounting and then it took on a face, the face of Mr. Phaeton DeSoto, the happy, smiling, effusive, in-your-face face of Mr. Phaeton DeSoto. Before her second foot touched the rug of Fellowship Hall, he was asking her advice about a troublesome kid in his junior high school class. He spoke with a voice that could be heard down the street, gesturing dramatically with his arms, touching her every second sentence, nothing improper but damned irritating none the

less. And then he would stare into her eyes until she answered his weekly query. Ugh, she shivered just to think of it. As she was answering, he
interrupted her with another concern urgently clamoring for expression.
Couldn't he even do her the courtesy of listening, she fumed inwardly.
Finally, he left her to the remnants of the cookie plate and the last-to-
leave members of the church! She was glad the coffee was gone. She
needed Valium more than caffeine. She sighed. No visitors greeted.
No deacons coordinated with. No friends talked to. Ugh, I'm an angry
wreck and he's skipping out the door. And yet DeSoto had been the only
one to volunteer to teach the junior high class she had been so eager to
launch. He was faithful and clearly committed to his faith. The teens
didn't seem to mind. Guilt welled up in Cabriolet. How could she be
angry at such a dependable Christian? What's wrong with me? Double
sigh.

Recourses for Transformation

"So that's what happened last Sunday at coffee hour and that's how I felt
about it. Not very Christian, huh?" Cabriolet put down her tea cup. It
was nice of Stanley Steamer to listen so attentively. He was in his late
seventies and the wise old grandfather of the congregation. He remembered everything and held it all in constructive perspective.

"Well, the first thing to do is chuckle a bit. I had the same struggles
with Phaeton a decade ago when he first joined the church and tried to
reshape the Trustee Board. I weren't too pleased, being the chairman at
the time. But we hung in there and survived. I even came to respect
him, and now I get a big kick outta him."

"Me, too, see my loose teeth?"

"Well, put yourself in his shoes a moment. He probably thinks we
are as frozen as a Norwegian fjord on New Year's Day. What with all
our quiet, simple, inanimate conversation. We must appear lifeless to
him. He was raised in a culture that values spontaneous, loud, sincere if
fleeting, expression. For him the immediate is real, and what pops into
his mind is the major part of the universe at that moment. It took me a
while to separate his style from his soul. But his soul is as big as his
gesturing. He really loves you or he wouldn't exert all this effort that is
getting your goat. He'd do anything for the church and God's people."

"Yeah, and that makes me feel guilty. He is a giving a person and I feel I should like him, but I just don't."

"No, need to like him. Liking occurs when you feel comfortable, not threatened, when you see yourself in the other person and so like what you see. When you like someone you are really liking yourself. That feels good and makes for enjoyable company, but it's not required. What's required of Christians is to love one another. And love is simply actively seeking the best for the other person."

"So, Stanley, you're saying I don't need to sweat liking Phaeton, I just need to sweat loving him?"

"Right, Cabriolet," Stanley chuckled. "It's not that hard, really. Phaeton actually expects you to be assertive with him; when you aren't, he tries all the harder to communicate with you."

"How can I assert when he constantly interrupts me?"

"Interrupt his interrupting. Phaeton grew up fighting for airtime. Just be honest. 'Phaeton, I hate it when you interrupt me. It makes me feel like I'm not really here. So hush up and listen for a minute. If you don't like what I have to say, I'll gladly refund your time!' Owning your reactions like that will get you a lot forwarder than withdrawing or blowing up and accusing him of insensitivity."

"Well, maybe."

"Maybe, is OK, too. After all, Jesus did not conduct an intimate in-depth ministry with hundreds of people. Just the twelve. And one of those was a skunk. Some people think it was just the Three. At some point you will come to peace with ministering to people at different levels. Peace or a nervous breakdown. What's the point of trying to be more Christ than Jesus was?"

On the way home Cabriolet was lost in thought, devising a strategy for Sunday's coffee hour. By the time she pulled into her driveway, she was downright anticipating it.

Resources for Further Study

Hall, Edward, *The Silent Language*, Garden City, New York: Doubleday, 1959.

Tannen, Deborah, *That's Not What I Meant: How Conversational Style Makes or Breaks Relationships*, New York: Simon and Schuster, 1991.

Temperaments and Personality Types

Forces at Work

Ever since Hippocrates it has been proposed that the whole human race could be categorized into personality types, usually four. (Hippocrates' four were sanguine, choleric, melancholic, and phlegmatic, based on which of the four body fluids predominated in a given individual: blood, phlegm, yellow, or black bile!) It seems that the next significant advance in personality type thinking occurred shortly after the turn of the twentieth century with such notable psychologists as Jung, Adler, Adickes, Kretschmer, and Spranger each proposing a new wrinkle on Hippocrates' theme. It took the world a while to recover from (or was it discover) all this erudition, but in the 1950s Isabel Myers and Katheryn Briggs devised a type indicator that seemed to scientifically apply personality type theory to individuals and collectives in a useful way. It became immensely popular. Almost everyone has heard of the Myers-Briggs Type Indicator test and most of us can, in four letters, reveal the essence of our being.

Myers and Briggs based their indicator test on the psychological theories of Jung.[1] Jung asserted that each human being had a preferred position on each of four pairs of indicators. He called these four pairs Extraversion (E) – Introversion (I), Sensing (S) – Intuitive (N), Thinking (T) – Feeling (F), and Perceiving (P) – Judging (J). Jung did not claim that a person was positioned only on one point on each of these pairs, but on both to some degree. Jung did not believe these preferences to be fixed, but potentially dynamic over time. The origin of a particular person's preferences is an open question. (You nature-nurture debaters can have a field day!) Jung believed one's preferred functions grow stronger with use and weaker with disuse.

So Jung bequeathed to us a schema of sixteen personality types. He apparently preferred the term preference, which I also prefer on theological grounds, because it gives place to volition and growth! Yet at any point in time one's type is a major descriptor of how one will act in the world. One's type describes one's preferred way of being and doing. It indicates one's "approach" to life, the kinds of activites one will chooose to engage in, and how one will perform those activities. Well, what are they?

Let us consider briefly each of the four pairs.

The E-I pair refers to more than shyness or confidence in public. Rather it indicates whether one gains energy from being with people (E) or by being with one's self and/or a few close friends (I).

The N-S pair refers to how one prefers to process the wild and wooly world beyond the self. The S preferer likes to deal with the data of his or her senses, facts, and directly accessible experiences. The N preferer likes to deal with schema that integrate facts, possibilities, metaphors and intuitions.

The T-F pair separates those who prefer an impersonal basis of choice (T) from those who prefer a personal basis (F). So an extreme F would decide to do something because it feels right to him or because of its positive ramifications for people he cares for. The T person would decide to do something because it is the right thing to do or because it is logical, efficient, necessary to preset goals, has a positive cost-benefit ratio, etc. The T person uses objective criteria while the F person uses subjective.

The P-J pair has to do with how one wants the world around oneself to be. The J prefers the world to be clear, fixed, orderly, and dependable. The P wants to live in a world of options, flexibility, surprises, and some richness of ambiguity. The J prefers to be sailing into a harbor; the P prefers to be sailing out of that harbor. The P would just as soon play, but the J has got to work!

A little quick math will show you that this results in sixteen distinguishable personality types: ESTP, ESTJ, ESFP, ESFJ, etc. Now this is all very helpful. It has reduced a world of five billion people down to sixteen personality types. That is a big step toward comprehensability, but unfortunately, even sixteen is too big a variety for most of us to carry around in our heads (I read of a primal tribe whose entire mathematics consists of 1, 2, 3, many; mine consists of 1, 2, 3, 4, too many!), and not every congregational member or new trustee will submit to the 121-question Myers-Briggs test. (A briefer, self-scored version is also available.) Yes, that is the trumpet of the U.S. Cavalry you hear: Keirsey and Bates have come to the rescue! The authors, psychologists, and trainers, have done two things to help us. First, they have created the Keirsey Temperament Sorter, a seventy-question test that even the most recalcitrant member can usually be induced (or coerced) to take! (My limited experience with it indicates results consistent with the Myers-Briggs test.)

Second, and possibly more important, Keirsey and Bates[2] have reduced Jung's sweet sixteen personality types down to a Final Four! Finding Hippocrates body fluids too "arcane," they have for some reason known best to themselves elected to use four Greek Gods to typify their personality types: Apollo, Dionysius, Prometheus, and Epimetheus. (Now I'm Greek and these are probably relatives of mine, but I'm not sure, K&B, that you've gotten beyond arcane-ness yet!)

Oh, well, because their book is so helpful, let's stick with their un-arcane personifications and get on with a little character study. K&B base their four-fold personality typing on Jung's N-S pairing. Apparently, they feel that this is the most fundamental in distinguishing personalities.

The Dionysian Temperament (SP)

If Dionysians had a motto it would be Free To Do! These SPs are ex-periential and open-ended. They do not prepare for tomorrow, they act today. Action, immediate and compelling, captures them. It is doing not duty that they act out. When life gets boring they bolt, confining they cop out. Places, people, or promises can be let go without a backward glance. The excitement of the moment is the ultimate value. They can get lost in their doing and be very creative or productive, but they can't endure today for a better tomorrow. Now is *all*. Dionysian types are impulsive and spontaneous, process oriented and playful, active but prone to wander, fraternal and generous, and particularly prone to the grand gesture. They will leap before they look, but their optimism al-ways counts on luck to pull them through. If not, easy come, easy go.

The Epimethean Temperament (SJ)

As Epimetheus stood by his wife Pandora and was left with loyalty and hope, so Epimetheans live to be useful to the social groupings they are part of. Belonging is crucial to the SJ, a belonging earned by their con-tinuous contribution to the good of the whole. As the SP desires freedom and independence, so the SJ desires connection and obligation. SJs "believe in" hierarchy, rules, and work. The SJ tends toward pessimism and cannot fathom the SPs unwarranted optimism. The SJ "ant" and the

SP "grasshopper" play out Aesop's fable eternally with the ending often intact; the ant takes the grasshopper in out of the cold—until spring, of course. For the SJ the social unit often becomes an end in itself. So tradition, heritage, duty, and service are high on his list. The SJ is society's saver, but SPs, spending freely on life, keep the relational economy going. Disapproval of transgressors is often followed by forgiveness, but sometimes the SJs forbidding nature is more visible. Despite feeling unappreciated, the SJ may take on ever increasing responsibilities. So the SJs elect vocations with high elements of service to others in the context of established institutions. SJs stabilize society, yet their contribution is never enough in their own eyes, and so they seek ever new levels of giving.

The Promethean Temperament (NT)

The Promethean personality is characterized by a desire for power, not power in a political or dictatorial manner, but as power over one's abilities in one's area of expertise, i.e., competence. The NT is driven to be able to understand, control, predict, and explain the significant realities around her. NTs frequently find themselves alone in a general group because they comprise such a small percentage of the total population. (For example, a group of thirty-two people would contain only one introverted NT.) And yet the NT is alone with himself, too, subjecting himself to ruthless self-criticism. The NT tests all theories and trusts no pronouncements. She can seem extremely individualistic and arrogant to others. Yet the NT is subject to self-doubt and a sense of inadequacy. As the SP sees work as play, the NT sees play as work, precisely scheduling fun and demanding of herself a good time! The NT experiences a further sense of isolation from others because of two conflicting messages the NT sends out and the resulting sense of intellectual inadequacy others feel in the presence of the NT. The messages are: I expect very little from you as I alone am competent, and I expect you to perform at the same demanding standard I use for myself! The NT is often quiet, fearing to bore others with obvious statements. The NT is always interested in Why? and likes to build models, bandy ideas, and develop systems. He must change the world around himself. The future is of preeminent importance, for bringing into being what might be. The NT feels that he deals with others honestly and straightforwardly, but is often perceived as cold, remote, and puzzling. NTs seldom register emotional dimensions of an interpersonal relation and often will analyze what they are experiencing rather than experiencing it. Sometime they are removed from life, watching it go by at a distance.

The Apollonian Temperament (NF)

The Apollonian quest is the Search for Self. The NF pursues the goal of becoming. The goals of the other three temperaments seem shallow and false compared to her thirst for self-actualization. Attaining his unique identity is the only place true fulfilment is to be found. All of life, all that one does, must contribute to his life's meaning. To an NF life is a drama, each circumstance offering the possibility of meaning. Of all the types, the NF can pick up on the most subtle clues, sometimes attributing to them much more meaning than is really there! NFs engage in relationships with a cyclical pattern. Positive expectations result in the expending of considerable effort in a relationship that never quite lives up to the potential of what could have been. NFs have a sense of mission, can speak and write clearly and distinctly, but project the search for meaning as incumbent on all personality types, often to the mystification if not the consternation of the others! NFs enjoy work that transmits ideas and attitudes to others, and "midwifing" others into becoming more human. The NF loves to be in contact and communication with others, but is often mistaken for what is in the eye of the beholder. Like the SP, the Apollonian wants to imbibe all the fullness of life, but always searches for meaning beyond the event itself. Like the NT, the NF looks to the future, in order that the potential of persons might be realized. Like Apollo, the NF seeks to link the human and the divine, resulting in a life-long process of becoming one's true self.

Sources of Stress

A world of only SPs would never make it through the winter; a world of only SJs would be pretty dull; a world of only NTs would be quite lonely; and a world of only NFs would hardly be this worldly at all. The

differences between types contribute to the fullness of humanity and to
the richness of life. The first source of stress in this area is the attitude
that the rest of humanity is, or ought to be, like me. This expectation
soon gets crossed with the reality that persons and personality types are
different. Because of the naive assumption of sameness, all manner of
frustration, irritation, projection of evil, and nonfunctionality are visited
on interpersonal relationships.

If I had to guess, I would say that my congregation is predominantly
composed of SJs, with a significant minority of NTs, and but a smatter-
ing of SPs and NFs. If I had a nickel for each time an SJ or NT referred
to one of our SPs as lazy, undisciplined, or a loser, or one of our NFs as
spacey, out there, or impractical, I could easily retire our congregation's
indebtedness! I am an NT and I truly value SJs, for they help to build
and then preserve what I have envisioned! The SPs are harder for me to
value for I can never get anywhere with them. It feels to me that all their
motion is in reality commotion! They are active but never seem to move
forward. Similarly, the NFs, although theoretically aligned, are difficult
to make a part of the team. They either see the congregation as lacking
in spirituality, or are happily off tilting at their newest internal windmill.
Both are, in my perspective, consumers of the congregation's life and
energy and it is hard to build (a good NT goal) with resources already
expended! I'd rather fight an SJ any day! And I have many days, for
although we may cross on specifics, e.g., preservation vs. innovation, we
both have the good of the whole in mind. The energies I cross with SPs
and NFs are so pervasive–affecting goals, life stances, perspectives, and
vocabulary–that sometimes it is a major task simply to put our differences on the table.

Yet I have expended a significant amount of pastoral energy to keep
the SP and NF personality types (particular people) in the central arena
of congregational life. It has not always been an easy task because then I
am shot at, as I mentioned earlier, by both groups. But it is important to
keep this stress alive in the life of my congregation for two reasons. The
first is that it is functional. The SP is light years ahead of the congregation as a whole in generosity. He is willing to give away his supper if a
need arises, as he has done (with the church, in the form of our discre-
tionary fund, charging to his rescue!). His example of selfless giving
will, I trust, someday infect the congregation as a whole. Similarly, the
NF continuously calls us to greater sensitivity to God's presence in our

midst, calling for healing services, sharing at worship to a level considered eyebrow-raising by the good SJs in the congregation, etc. Of course, when the NF's calls convict the Deacons and we start a prayer/share group, for example, she is off attending a seminar in Oshkosh!! Still she keeps us looking at the ways we can grow spiritually.

The second reason has to do with the fullness of the Godhead in human society. I suppose that psychologists on the basis of the evidence available would type Jesus as an NF. But Jesus did not complete God's intention for humanity. That is, Jesus was not enough, for God's final plans include us, too. Jesus was the first principle, the engendering spirit, the Child of God among many siblings! Otherwise, God would have quit this drama we call humanity no later than the ascension. The infinite God cannot be contained in finitude, but a part of the infinite God is reflected in each faithful personality. All the parts help us to better ascertain the whole. In other words, Jesus needs you if God's character is to be more fully incarnated in human experience. And I need each of my brothers and sisters in Christ if God's presence is to be more fully realized on Block Island. Those SPs and NFs might drive me nuts, but it is a divine insanity.

If the first source of stress results from our response to personality types that conflict with ours, the second stress results from personality types that too neatly complement ours. Because any one personality type is an incomplete expression of humanity, humans seek to fill the void, sometimes in a healthy manner, but too often in a form of codependency. The SP grasshopper soon realizes that the ant will always take him in, and so declines to temper his preferences with the real needs of life. Correspondingly the ant, needing to be needed, has a nice little dysfunction going with the grasshopper: all summer he is able to carp at him about preparing for the winter and all winter tell him so, while steadfastly ignoring where his preferences, unchecked by Christ's call to grow to maturity, have placed him. Or the NT may marry an SP to bring spice into his life without having to learn how to play or be playful. The NF may hook up with an SJ to make sure the rent is paid, etc.

In these interpersonal relationships stress results from the crossing of energy between the inertia of a personality type and the spiritual demands of the environment to mature. This stress is a silent killer because it feels like a solution. Realizing it feels more like a problem than the problem itself, and dealing with it seems more stressful than letting sleeping dogs lie. But those same sleeping dogs will always wake and then, well rested, will turn and attack their "master." Less stress is generated by dealing with them to begin with. Interpersonal complementarity is the healthy form of which codependency is the dysfunctional form. It is a matter of balance and degree. And, fortunately, others have written eloquently on this. (See Resources.)

Recourses for Transformation

To turn personality type related stress (crossed energy) into aligned energy three actions will be helpful: acknowledge, appreciate, and compensate.

Acknowledge. Volitionally and joyously give up the idea that everyone is alike and they are all like you. God made each of us different to reflect a portion of the infinite riches of the divine personality. So accept it and rejoice in it. Humble yourself by acknowledging what an impoverished world this would be if everyone was just like you! Then tell your church leaders about your conversion and invite them to join you in repentance. Of course, first you have to "type" yourself. In reviewing personality typing in order to write this section, I relearned that I am a strong NT, with a good bit of SJ and a little bit of NF and almost no SP. This goes a long way in explaining why our church works so hard, has to schedule fun, and, even without my "help," overorganizes it. And it explains why I get along so well with certain people in the church and less well with others. As other church members get a handle on their "type," similar insights will surface for them, and their ability to respect others as simply different will increase.

Appreciate. I worked on a project a while back with a friend. Inadvertently, I annoyed him by responding to virtually all of his suggestions with, "I don't have a problem with that." I thought I was accepting his suggestions. But he didn't want me to not have a problem; he wanted my enthusiastic ownership or to show him why not. So, too, with personality types, mere acceptance is but the beginning of releasing and realigning energies. Appreciation must follow. Let us conceive of the local congregation metaphorically as a baseball team. (The theological legitimacy of this awaits complete articulation. For now, just trust me!) Every squad that hopes to get somewhere wants to have a couple of jackrabbits, a couple of thumpers, some folk who can throw leather, and some who can throw heat, etc. Each player has his unique strength to contribute to a facet of the game. Nine home run hitters is a ticket to the cellar, just as surely as an all pitch no hit team (witness Boston and Detroit in recent years). So, too, in the Body of Christ greater health is achieved by the full spectrum of personality types, each contributing from his or her storehouse. My SP friend whom I mentioned earlier might try my patience, but, for example, no one else in the congregation gives up a week's salary to coach the baseball week at our denomination's camp each summer. He and his wife just keep on giving and that example has a necessary place in our corporate life.

Compensate. Just as we can appreciate the strengths of each personality type, so also can we compensate for the weaknesses of each. We try to keep our NFs off the Trustee Board, but represented on the Deacon Board. If we place a lot of SPs and NFs as Sunday School teachers, it is nice to have an SJ as Superintendent. Personality types should not be blamed for doing poorly what they can't do well. They should be compensated for by the wise and loving leadership of the congregation.

And personally, this approach is functional also. A true statement like this will go over well with all but the most defensive: "Sally, I really appreciate that out of your Godgiven personality you can do (X) so well. And aren't we both glad that Susie is around to do (opposite of X) which is her gift."

Resources for Further Study

Beattie, Melodie, *Codependent No More,* Center City, MN: Hazelden, 1987.

Edwards, Lloyd, *How We Belong, Fight, and Pray: The MBTI as a Key to Congregational Dynamics*, Washington, DC: The Alban Institute, 1993.

Jung, Carl G., *Man and His Symbols,* New York: Dell Publishing, 1964.

Keirsey, David and Marilyn Bates, *Please Understand Me, Character and Temperament Types*, Del Mar, CA: Prometheus Nemesis Book Company, 1978.

Kroeger, Otto and Janet M. Thuesen, *Type Talk: The 16 Personality Types that Determine How We Live, Love and Work,* New York: Dell Publishing, 1988.

Oswald, Roy M., and Otto Kroeger, *Personality Type and Religious Leadership,* Washington, DC: The Alban Institute, 1988.

Schaef, Anne Wilson and Diane Fassel, *The Addictive Organization,* San Francisco: Harper and Row, 1988.

Transactional Analysis

Forces at Work

In his book *Games People Play*[3], Eric Berne popularized an approach to interpersonal comunication patterns. This approach theorizes that at any given moment in a social context an individual will exhibit one of three ego states. These three states are labelled Parent, Adult, and Child. The Parent represents communication learned from parental figures that help in the actual parenting of children and also routines, rituals, and traditions that represent both the way we do things and the way we ought to do things. The Adult processes data and makes decisions that allow for effective dealing with the outside world. The Child is the repository of intuition, play, spontaneity, fun, and creativity. All three ego states contribute to the communication of a healthy person.

Berne symbolized the individual person as a snowman of three circles, Parent, Adult, and Child from top to bottom. To analyze a conversation Berne faces two snowmen representing the two speakers and then draws an arrow from the ego state that is the source of the first "transaction" to the intended receiving ego state. The second party to the conversation then responds with an arrow of their own. These arrow sequences can be charted and the resulting transactions analyzed. Thus Berne's approach is labelled Transactional Analysis.

Pairs of arrows that align are called complementary transactions. So a Parent-Parent transaction might be one in which two people lament the current behavior of the teenagers in town. An Adult-Adult transaction might involve two deacons analyzing why attendance is up or down. A Child-Child transaction might involve a creative idea for a game to play followed by a spontaneous squeal of pleasure to get started. Complementary transactions can also occur with different ego states in the two speakers as when a Parental arrow of protection elicits a Child arrow of appreciation.

Sources of Stress

This is all well and good and boring as long as conversation proceeds in a complementary way. What makes it interesting for our purposes is when a "crossed transaction" occurs. A crossed transaction is a communication in which the two arrows cross in the diagram (as well as in real life!). Thus a constructive criticism regarding the length of the sermon (Adult to Adult) is heard as an insult and responded to with an arrow of defensiveness (Child to Parent) "Well, if you weren't late all the time it wouldn't seem so short." Or, with an arrow of superciliousness (Parent to Child), "Who are you, a mere layman to critique me, graduated first in my class from Harvard Divinity School?" Berne says it is a rule that with crossed transactions communication breaks off.

Berne adorns his analysis with many bells and whistles, such as describing rituals, procedures, and games and varying levels of meaning **in transaction, social, and psychological.** But his basic model gives us enough to get a handle on much crossed energy in our congregations. These crossed transactions can be counted on to generate irritation, frustration, and confusion. Aggressive or distancing behavior is a typical further response.

A crossed transaction "game" that we identify in our congregation is "Help Me." It goes like this:

Pastor on phone: Is coffee hour all set? It's your week, you know. *(Adult-Adult)*
Dazed Deacon: Today? Oh, yeah. Oh, my. Could you help me please? The dog is loose. My husband is playing volleyball and my

car is stuck crossways in the road. Just plug in the coffee pot and I'll do the rest when I get to church. *(Helpless Child to Rescuing Parent!)*

Recourses for Transformation

1. **Understanding** that we each operate out of ego states is the first step in transforming crossed energy. When arrows cross we can take a step back and be understanding of the misalignment rather than unreflectively glaring or getting upset.

2. **Choose.** We can at any moment choose which ego state we wish to operate out of and which we wish to target in the other. If we don't like how the transaction is going we can rewrite at least our half of the script. One afternoon last week I spent four sweaty hours chopping up the old wood floor from a deck I had replaced for firewood to help my family make it through the severity of our New England winters. I did not expect the Congressional Medal of Honor, and a good thing, too, because I didn't get it, not even close. Instead, my wife sent a Parental to Child arrow: "If you really cared about me and the children, you wouldn't burn old, painted wood." I launched a flurry of Adult to Adult arrows describing the extent of my caring, the airtightness of our stove, the ecological impact of burning vs. landfilling, etc. Counter Parent arrows were soon airborne remarking on my blatant, self-preoccupied overlooking of all the smoke our "airtight" stove filled the house with, etc. No sooner had we each retreated to a neutral corner than I realized my mistake: I cross-communicated. I could have rewritten the transaction with aligned communication. I could have replied impishly, "I do care about you, dear; it's this old wood I could do without." Or, "Oh darn, now I'll have to come up with another scheme to do you guys in." Or, "Not to worry, honey, I will only burn this wood when I'm alone." Child's play. I could have rewritten my script, and I will next time. I promise.[4]

3. **Patience**. Most of us have "default" ego states, the one that we prefer to use. Appropriateness is learned over time. In the meantime, patience helps.

4. **Change by reflection**. Gently holding up childish arrows in the "Help Me" game will allow people to see themselves as others see them. They may choose to change or not, but at least they won't be trapped unknowingly in a transaction pattern that doesn't work.

Resources for Further Study

Eric Berne, *Games People Play*, New York: Grove Press, 1964.

Coping with Alligators

Forces at Work and Sources of Stress

The frustration of the expectation that others will have the same style of interpersonal interaction, the same assumptions about relationships, similar personality preferences and psychological postures results in significant levels of stress. But pastors who are experiencing the next level of interpersonal stress would gladly trade back for those good old days when stress was "only" at those levels. This next level of interpersonal stress cuts to the heart, threatens one's job and even one's sanity, and can plunge one into heartache and despair at unprecedented levels.

Pastors who have experienced this level of interpersonal stress describe their protagonists in clear and unflattering terms. One calls them alligators, "toothy ferocious looking predators waiting furtively to snap up the unwary pastor as he or she passes by."[5] Another pastor rejects the terms "character, thorn, burden, difficult, problem," in favor of the term "church killer."[6] A pastoral counsellor is even more explicit. He decribes these people as "clergy killers." He says, "Clergy killers are evil. They do evil intentionally, and willingly pursue its destructive means and ends. Even repentance is typically a tactic only . . . There are clinical names . . . personality disorders, paranoid, antisocial, borderline, histrionic, narcissistic, and passive aggressive. They may be previous or present victims of abuse. They may have volatile or addictive personalities. They may have inadequate socialization, arrested adolescence, and violent role models. They may have developed a perverse, voyeuristic, and vindictive taste for the suffering of their victims. [Church Killers] have learned the power of throwing tantrums . . . They know how to be bullies."[7]

It is truly said that hurt people hurt people. And it is true that pastors are not always innocent victims either. Some pastors are hurtful person-alities and some bring their own fuel to their fire. Nevertheless, pastors often find themselves in a relationship that is destructive, painful, and chronic. Pastors are frequently surprised by this phenomenon. Yet we should expect it. By and large congregations are made up of warm, lov-ing, and tolerant Christians. And just for that reason people with power needs or other pathologies find the church a viable environment to act out their internal illness. Ideally, the congregation will react in respon-sible ways to transform or at least contain the harmful behavior. (We will touch on this more in the next chapter.) However, that would be an ex-ceptional congregation. More often churches are unskilled or unmoti-vated to call people to account. So the pastor will need to deal with his or her stress in the midst of destructive relationships.

Recourses for Transformation

Jesus tells the story of the king who would wage war but upon tallying the strength of his army decides instead to sue for peace. The pastor who is experiencing interpersonal hostility to the point of deep personal stress needs also to "tally the strength of his or her army." Who is on your side? Who is in your support system—spouse, family, extended family, clergy colleagues, friends in the congregation, denominational connec-tions, professional counsellors, friends outside the congregation, etc.? This is a political question. The answer to it will have significant impli-cations on the recourses open to the pastor. But it is more than a political question. It is also a stress capacity question. The pastor with a vital system of support may be able to "take a licking and keep on ticking," whereas the pastor with a nonexistent or undeveloped support system is liable to be shredded by the first alligator that comes along. Is there enough time, energy, and opportunity to build a support system even in the midst of interpersonal hostility?

One of the insidious dynamics of clergy killers is an ability to create a high enough level of stress and anxiety within the pastor so that the

pastor engages in self-defeating behaviors giving apparent confirmation
to the clergy killer's distrust of the pastor. The clergy self-destructs.
Decisions made in places of defensiveness, reactionary and paranoid
places, are low quality decisions. For example, the pastor misjudges the
reaction of the congregation to the accusations of the alligator. Instead
of ignoring them, confident in the congregation's trust, he is threatened
by them and, by attempting to rebut them, adds credence instead. Or she
reads the congregation's questioning as accusation when it was really a
search for data to rebut the accusations, and so withdraws into silence
when open conversation was indicated. Accurately reading one's position relative to the alligator and the social group is difficult business and
can only be done from a safe place. Decisions made from other than a
safe place will tend to be low quality decisions and are likely to have a
deleterious effect.

I vividly remember an incident in our town that was very stressful
to me. Our church trustees were attempting to finalize a fifty-year-old
bequest that left some residual land to the church and a local conservation group. The trustees didn't see any need to communicate the
church's position personally when they had such an articulate pastor.
Naive and so seduced, I presented the church's claim, not to acclamation
but to opposition. The opposition to "me" was led by a very powerful
young woman who felt that the conservation group of which she was a
member ought to receive the bulk of the land. I was astounded to find
all these legal wranglings on the front page of the local newspaper! As
the going got tougher I was convinced that the whole town was aligned
against me and the church. I felt this to be true to the point that at a
league basketball game I was sure everyone was avoiding me. I felt
isolated and alone. The next day at midweek Bible study an occasion
arose and I shared this feeling. A church member who was also at the
game look confused, and then commented, "But when you scored your
basket everyone cheered. You got the biggest hand of anyone." (Note:
"your basket," singular. I score baskets at such a rate that each one is
cause for celebration, an event comparable in frequency to the arrival of
Haley's comet.) It was only then—twenty-four hours later—that I
"heard" the cheers. I was so convinced that people were against me, I
was in such a harsh place, that I could not register reality, and could very
easily have made self-destructive decisions from there. Fortunately, the
safe place of my fellow studiers allowed me a new, objective, and

constructive place from which to assess my position. It is imperative to find a safe place where the power of the interpersonal hostility cannot reach, and only there make decisions.

The first decision is summarized in the phrase fight or flight. Fleeing has some merit as a stress reducer, at least in the short run. Some pastors make a career of "honeymoon only" pastorates. As soon as the first interpersonal hostility surfaces they are "outta there." Some stress is thus avoided but a lot of growth, personal and congregational, is forgone. Still there are times when flight is not only the desirable but also the most viable option. If the clergy killer is a central member of the congregation and has the support of the majority, then they have chosen to be codependent with his or her illness and the pastors who stay to fight will undoubtedly end up being crucified, not leading the congregation into a promised land. If the interpersonal cost to the pastor is too high, if there are physical or psychological reasons to avoid this level and duration of stress, if a realistic assessment of congregational change would require three of four miracles, if the pastor could countenance a short fight but not a long one, then relocating is probably consistent with the will of God.

If as pastor you choose to fight on, an assessment must be made of the alligator's nature. Some people are temporary alligators, acting mean and nasty as a response to a passing trauma in their lives. Time will defang them (until the next trauma?). But it is a deeper level of interpersonal hostility that we are focusing on here. There are three possible postures of clergy killers: he is trapped in an alligator suit and would like to be released if he only knew how; she is an alligator chameleon only turning into an alligator under certain definable circumstances; or he is a proactive alligator, unhappy unless he can eat the pastor for supper. A different set of responses is appropriate for each situation. Again, having a safe place to decide which tack to take is imperative. Of course, interpersonal relations are dynamic and the situation can change midstream, escalate or ameliorate. The savvy pastor can always mix and match elements from each of these three general strategies.

A. "Kiss me and I'll Turn into a Prince"

Vicious interpersonal behavior can be a cry for help. If so, these steps may prove transformative. They were distilled in the midst of struggle.

I have adapted them from the reflections of Michael Kroll, a pastor
friend of mine in Vermont.[8]

1. Use pastoral teaching and preaching opportunities to paint a picture
of healthy, Christ-like interpersonal behavior. Preaching at people, of
course, is unlikely to transform hurtful relationships. But words do have
power. Biblical injunctions and examples, the lifting up of healthy behavior of other church members, stories or how-to's of healthy conflict
resolution or reconciliation can at least "soften up" the "enemy." (Oops,
excuse my military jargon.)

2. Engage in active listening, clarification. Most communication difficulties arise from hearing what you thought was said instead of hearing
what the other person thought he was saying! Active listening is the skill
of rephrasing the communication of the other person until she concurs
that her thought has been communicated. When two people start on very
different wavelengths, this can be quite a difficult endeavor. But this
process of clarification can avert much heartache later on. Yesterday one
of my Sunday School teachers told me about the fight he didn't have!
He had, unobserved, overheard his basketball coach lamenting about
their team's poor showing and specifically calling him "half a man."
He was about to prove just how macho a man he was by acting like an
adolescent and popping his coach, when further conversation revealed
the coach's meaning: with his bunged up knees he could only play at
half capacity!

3. Always test reality and help others to do so, too. Each of us assumes
that our take on reality *is* reality. We forget about the limitations on our
input and processing, our preset ideas, our filters, our pre-existing constructs. It is a wonder that any of us is in contact with reality at all! In
my basketball story, it took me nearly twenty-four hours to hear the ap-
plause; I had built an illusory reality of isolation and avoidance that was
so strong it precluded my registering objective events! Many alligator
bites are over misinterpretations of events. Ask others. Find out the
view of noninvolved people. Check out your assumptions. Invite others
to do so, too.

4. Help people restate their positions into postures with transformative
potentials. Actively listening means working until you really hear what

the other person is saying. Restating is helping people to hear what they aren't saying! Sometimes hostile statements mask emotions that are too hot to handle. Restating puts that emotion on the table to look at and implicitly says that it is OK, at least as a starting point. I counsel with an elderly lady who vehemently showers her sister with abuse and expends enormous energy describing to me all the ways in which her sister sins against her. Finally, I could say, "You feel you are the victim of your sister's actions, and you feel powerless to change things except by vilifying her." The potential for transformation has now entered the relationship. Restating is also a way of reframing the communication. A key board member called me with anxiety in her voice. She had just spoken with former member Y who was hurt by Chairman X. "This isn't the first time he's done this. Pretty soon negative repercussions will be felt throughout the congregation." (I was privy to the whole developing "hurt" and knew, unfortunate as it was, we would all be OK with it.) "It is true Mr. X is very goal oriented and ofttimes doesn't tune into the feelings of others," I responded. "But he is sincere and dependable and does a lot of good. Maybe as we work together on the board we can help him factor in feelings, too." By accepting this new formulation, Mr. X had been transformed from a virus to a fellow journeyer, if not a reclamation project!

5. Invite the protagonist to swap shoes for a mile. The scar in my memory is still visible, if not tender, from an episode about eight years ago at our Executive Board. I had been pastoring on Block Island about a decade and had also, recently, accepted a number of speaking engagements across the country. I was aware of the pressure this put on my schedule and the tension of not being as present on the island. But I was totally blindsided by the accusation of one of the Board members. He accused me of duplicity, using my speaking at small church conferences as a cover for trying to find a bigger church!!

First of all, I am not bright enough to think up such a Machiavellian strategy. (Maybe that was part of the hurt!) Second, I thought myself a person of too much integrity to engage in an ongoing strategy of deceit, and I was deeply hurt to be accused of such! When I picked my mouth up off the floor, I reminded him of the insularity of island life; I explained the deepening of my thought necessitated by preparing for those speaking engagements. I mentioned the new ideas I received in the company of other pastors and committed laypeople, and the churches benefit by having a growing, not stagnant, pastor. Maybe for the first time he caught a glimpse of the view from my side of things, and became much more accepting of me and the limitations in our setting. Just about that time I suffered a yearlong bout with Lyme disease. I endured disruptions on the physical, mental, and emotional levels. I was forced to relinquish some of my "can-do" whippersnapperness, and accept a "there but by the grace of God, go I" attitude toward my life. And empathy as distinct from sympathy became a significant part of my being! My accuser had since boyhood endured a physical impairment that was beginning to accelerate in his more recent years. I had walked a year in his shoes and had ofttimes been frustrated, depressed, and accusatory. Maybe I should have been less hurt in reacting to his comment and more realizing that we were all hurting together!

6. Suggest counselling. Suggest counselling and duck! Or mediation or third party reconciliation. The young woman I mentioned earlier and I had become frozen in a standoff relative to the land distribution. A wise retired trustee called us both together. Though the atmosphere was so thick it could have been cut with a knife, we started to realize that this paralysis was beneficial to no one. We started to note common points. We were able to give a little and finally we found a way to resolve the land issue and we also found that our personality difficulties had spent themselves. I thank God she is now worshipping with us again. But without John's intervention, I shudder to think of the ongoing levels of pain!

B. "See What Fine Teeth I Have, My Dear"

Sometimes the alligators are content to remain alligators. Their vicious behavior is not a call for help but simply an expression of a fixated personality. Like real alligators they may be content to lie like a log on the pond's edge but only until provoked. A constructive pastoral posture towards these sleeping alligators may involve the following aspects. (These follow closely the learnings of Mike Ashcraft,[9] formerly pastor of a small church in Indiana.)

1. Maintain a "loving distance" from your alligators. Pastors do not have to be bosom buddies of each and every parishioner. In fact, only those pastors eager for a nervous breakdown should even try to be. So why not come to peace with some folk being on the outer circle of your ministry? And why not let those folk include the alligators? This does not mean being closed to deeper levels of future ministry. God may yet open doors that seem permanently closed. It simply means recognizing and accepting current reality.

2. Do not create camps. If the alligator snarls at you, do not try to protect yourself, as Jacob did in regard to Esau, with all the other members of your (spiritual) household. God subjected him to an all night wrestling match whereas I bet you could use some rest! The protection that you have is spiritual—your own spiritual maturity and the Christlike functioning of the congregation. Any attempt to recruit people to your side, actually weakens the Body of Christ. Either/or relational alternatives are inherently unstable and destructive. And they are not necessary, save possibly in extreme cases. Usually, the snarling can be ignored and ministry continued. Often the snarling alligator will be rendered irrelevant when the pastor simply lives and ministers by a higher set of rules. I crossed energies with a gentleman in our congregation (see Puppet section in the next chapter). Although his rejection of me and his hurtful behavior caused me much pain, I attempted to keep my pastoring and my relationships with everyone else on an even keel. Because the rest of the congregation and I were working in a fairly mutual manner and moving forward together, his voice became an increasingly distant one, fainter and fainter. Finally, he had no audience at all. Any attempt to array members around me against him would have enhanced his power and hurt Christ's body.

3. Keep your head down. One of the most spiritually liberating realizations of my pastoring has been that there is a Messiah and that he is not me! I don't have to fight every fight, climb every mountain, solve every problem, come up with every brilliant idea, and battle every alligator. Christ has a whole body to do his work. Yep, sometimes I have to take a stand and draw the line and even fight, but not every time. The rest of God's people are capable and gifted and empowered and deployed by God. Give them enough room to do God's maneuvering! Every once in

a while one of my deacons gets proud of the spiritual work he is doing, and raises his head heavenward and asks the Lord how he is doing, knowing full well the only answer. Whereupon he hears from heaven, "Put your head down and get back to work!" Good advice for each of us.

4. Remember part of me is alligator-esque! It is tempting to paint the alligator as all bad and oneself as all good. It is tempting, but it is self-delusion. There is some good and some bad in each of us. Even the most mature pastor has further growing to do. The "purpose" of the alligator may be to mirror those parts of ourselves that are not as loving, compassionate, and merciful as they need to be. I have been privileged to hear the cries of many pastors, heartfelt pain often inflicted by alliga-tors. But frankly, many of these alligators were prodded into action by aspects of the pastor's personality or performance that could be im-proved. That doesn't justify alligator behavior, but it does serve to alert the alligator-fighting pastor that his or her personality, perspective, or performance may also be in need of transformation. I have recorded elsewhere[10] both the battles and the blessings I received from what I took to be the prototypical alligator. I look back at the transformation in me as a result of our struggles, and I wouldn't give up that growth for anything.

5. Pray for the alligators. This is not easy. But prayer does change our attitudes. It is hard to spend all your energy in defending yourself when you are giving a significant portion to prayer for that person. Prayer not only brings us into God's presence, it also brings us into God's perspec-tive. And from God's point of view alligators look more like lost, needy, hurting souls, not essentially different from ourselves.

C. "I'm Gonna Get You!"

There are times when alligators are hell bent on your destruction. In his provocative article "Clergy Killers,"[11] Lloyd Rediger relates the horrify-ing story of three professors who connived in jealousy to destroy their successful pastor. The breakdown of his psyche, his vocational skills, and even his marriage were the results of their devilish work. Rediger concludes his article with some weapons of defense when proactive alligators attack.

1. Be aware of the existence of clergy killers. All is not light in the Kingdom of Light. Acknowledgement, not denial, is the appropriate response when facing the evil work of clergy killers. Some characteristics to note: clergy killers are not satisfied with a single victory; it is not the issue at hand but the destruction of the pastor that is their goal. Clergy killers do not leave the church after victory or defeat or in the midst of conflict; they may regroup or retrench or tactically retreat, but they don't abandon their work. And there is no satisfying them; as it was with Hitler, every concession is the basis of a new demand.

2. Educate the congregation to this pathology. This is difficult for the pastor under attack, for it may be seen as an unfair counterattack. Bring in third party resources, denominational people, consultants, pastoral counsellors. Their objectivity may help persuade the congregation of the seriousness of the situation.

3. Learn survival skills. Some or all of the following may help: A) praying, especially with the Psalms of David; B) obtaining counselling for personal support; C) mobilizing your political allies in the congregation; D) obtaining political support from the denomination; E) maintaining the moral high ground; and F) communicating so that the truth and your vision for ministry are in front of the congregation.

4. Educate yourself and key congregational leaders about the reasons and procedures for censure, removal, and/or excommunication of members. If you are truly dealing with cancer, surgical removal may be the only hope for survival. But remember two Pauline warnings: 1) Be innocent yourself (Galatians 6:1), and 2) the point of removal is not revenge, but repentance (II Thessalonians 3:14).

Resources for Further Study

Ashcraft, Mike, "Dealing with Difficult Church Members," *The Five Stones* (Winter 1987): 2-4.

Freeman, Joel A., *Dealing with the Wolves: Serpents and Swine in Your Life,* San Bernardino, CA: Here's Life Publishers, 1991.

Kroll, Michael, "Caring for the Family of God," *The Five Stones* (Fall 1991): 14-17.

Leas, Speed and Paul Kittlaus, *Church Fights: Managing Conflict in the Local Church,* Philadelphia: Westminster Press, 1973.

Leas, Speed, *Moving Your Church Through Conflict,* Bethesda, MD: The Alban Institute, 1985.

Oates, Wayne E., *The Care of Troublesome People,* Bethesda, MD: The Alban Institute, 1994.

Rediger, G. Lloyd, "Clergy Killers," *The Clergy Journal* (August 1993): 1-2.

Rediger, G. Lloyd, *Coping with Clergy Burnout,* Valley Forge, PA: Judson Press, 1982.

CHAPTER 4

Role-Related Stress

Introduction

Another arena of stress pastors are subject to is role-related. Role connotes an actor playing a part. In different branches of the Christian church, the pastoral role or office has been emphasized as distinct from the pastor as an individual person. Thus, in higher churches for example, the efficacy of the sacraments are not tied to the moral worthiness of the administrator. It is the role (as priest) not the person (who must by definition be a sinner) that imbues the performance of the sacrament with spiritual power. Lower church folk have had trouble with this understanding insisting that the pastoral role be more than "just play acting." There ought to be some consistency between the pastor *as* person and the pastor *as* pastor. (Thus our moral outrage at the behavior of the televangelists in recent years.) In a sociological understanding, role is seen as a set of behaviors that fulfill a specific function in an organization or society and are understood to be appropriate by both the person performing them and the persons receiving them.

It is not hard to see the tremendous potentials for stress in the arena of pastoral role. Stress can result in members of a congregation who don't know how to act, think, or feel when the life of their priest crosses with his or her "part" as Christ's vicar. Stress can result in the soul of the priest who compares his or her own life with the perfection of the role. (Remember what poor, young Martin Luther went through?) The stress we want to examine in greater detail, though, concerns the conflict of energy that results when role *definitions* are crossed. When both parties to a role transaction view it as appropriate, energies are aligned.

The mailman delivers the mail and the garbageman picks up the garbage. OK, no problem. But let the mailman deliver garbage and the garbageman trash our mail, we cease to be happy campers. (Hmm, given all the junk mail I just found stuffed in my mailbox, maybe that wasn't such a clear example!) If a powerful car marked "Police" with sirens blaring and flashers blazing pulls us over, and a uniformed man gets out and shows his badge, we may not be happy, but we accept the reality of the situation as a police officer doing his duty. My wife was once pulled off the road by a pick-up truck with stick-on flashers. A casually dressed man emerged and announced that he was an auxillary officer, and...We would all agree that there was something wrong with that picture! Especially in this day and age, it does not fit our definition of the role of a police officer.

Pastoral roles have their definitions, too. When the pastor acts out of a role definition that is consistent with the role definition held by the congregation, the members may not alway be happy, but stress, as we have defined it, does not result. However, should the pastor be acting out of one picture while the congregation is expecting the enactment of another, then stress results. The energies of the two parties have crossed in the arena of role definition. We will consider three levels of pastoral role stress: task, function, and symbolism.

The Pastoral Role as Task

Forces at Work

The pastoral role is multifaceted. A pastor is expected to function productively in solitary study, one on one relationships, family systems and small groups, and large, public settings. A pastor is expected to field historical, Biblical, theological, moral, psychological, sociological, administrative, and janitorial matters in a Golden Glove manner. In some ways a pastor is expected to be all things to all people. But even this "all things" bears some specification. A helpful delineation is offered by Margaret Fletcher Clark in *Ten Models of Ordained Ministry*.[1] She writes:

"There is no science more *un*scientific than figuring out what one expects of one's pastor. The complexity of that issue, and the trouble congregations get into when expectations get out of sync with what their pastor *is,* make this an issue of some importance."

Her ten models are as follows:

1. **Counselor/Healer/Caretaker**
    This ordained minister spends a major part of the week in pastoral counseling appointments in the church office and visiting at the hospital.
2. **Minister of the Word**
    An ordained minister of this model likes to preach and teach. Sermons usually include scriptural and/or theological exposition.
3. **Administrator/Manager of an Organization**
    This ordained minister resembles a corporate executive, one who manages a productive and effective organization.
4. **Prophet/Social Activist**
    This ordained minister is more often on the streets, in meetings, or calling on the mayor than in the church office. The excitement of living and working out there on the cutting edge of things seems to wipe out the litany of daily parochial concerns.
5. **Social Exemplar**
    In this model, both ordained minister and spouse come of socially acceptable families and are graduates of the better colleges. Their education is expressed in simple good taste, from food to literature to dress. Sermons can be depended on to point clearly to Christian behavior. In sum, a thoroughly dependable person.
6. **Ring Leader**
    This ordained minister has organized myriad small groups in the parish—working committees, Bible study, house, church, etc.—loosely knit together by an informal communication and referral system. Sunday morning is a madhouse.
7. **Community Personage**
    An ordained minister is the city's "first citizen," living into local traditions with unquestioned personal authority—active in community organization, saying an invocation at major civic events, etc.
8. **Celebrant**
    This ordained minister is most at home leading the congregation in worship. He or she loves ritual and ceremony, celebrates in infor-

mal as well as formal settings, and shares a rich knowledge of rites
and lore with enthusiasm and grace.

9. **Spiritual Guide**

    In this model, the ordained minister is one who encourages the de-
    velopment of spiritual life by all in the congregation.

10. **Witness**

    The ordained minister in this model reflects an infectious love of
    God, not so much by action as by presence. We might expand this
    model to include not only the witness of presence, but witnessing,
    too. So this pastor sees himself or herself as an evangelist or trainer
    of evangelists. Conversion and personal decision are key goals in
    many traditions.

Sources of Stress

There are three ways in which energies can cross in relation to task-
oriented pastoral role definitions. We might label these three: different,
insufficient, and inefficient.

Different. Stress results then when the pastor perceives himself or herself incarnating primarily one of these pastoral roles while the congregation expects a different one to be primary. Because most people do not
think in terms of roles and role definitions, and most pastors do not feel a
calling to an amorphous pastoral ministry but to their particular understanding or image of the pastoral ministry, much energy can be invested
in this crossing. Often this energy is expressed as personal conflict. The
pastor is failing (versus succeeding at a differtent role definition). Personal hurt, communication breakdown, entrenched battle lines, etc., often
are the marks of escalation. Pastors can feel blindsided by the revolt of
the congregation while they were, by their definition, doing a decent job
of ministry. Just what *do* these people want? Simply, they want to see a
different role enacted. The classic example is that of the young, ener-
getic, idealistic, urban-trained seminary grad being placed in a "first"
pastorate out in the country. His or her social activism based on his or
her vision of the kingdom is not only not appreciated, it is downright
derided. The congregation has made an artform of not rocking the boat;
they have learned that silence and survival have high overlap! They

want only to be loved and nurtured. But the pastor insists on tilting at windmills. Of course, any other two of these ten task definitions can cross and result in stress, also.

Insufficient. Actually most pastors have a pastoral role definition broad enough to include more than one of these models. They may have a lead model that they feel most comfortable with, but also two or three others that, though secondary, are natural roles. Some of the ten role definitions may feel alien or hypocritical to particular pastors. But some can be learned, or at least a minimal functionality can be acquired. Congregations, too, have a breadth of role definition. They can tolerate the enactment of some that are not central if some of the central ones are also in evidence.

Stress can also arise at a secondary level, even if the pastor and congregation are aligned on the primary task definition. This is so because the "pastoral role" is really a collection of roles. A pastor who could only perform one of the ten tasks listed above would be a one-dimensional, almost cardboard figure. I find the multifaceted role of the pastor satisfying. If one hat is difficult or boring, I can switch to another that I find more harmonious. But this switching is only functional if the congregation's and the pastor's energy are aligned about it. Alignment on the primary task only will result in a short-lived "honeymoon," with increasing stress over time. Of course, the priority of pastoral tasks vary across the membership and the task preference of the pastor tends to change over time, so there can be no such thing as a stress-free alignment of pastoral tasks over any length of time. Misalignment or crossed energies are constant potentials, especially on this secondary level.

You've heard of the congregation that unanimously agreed that their new pastor would be a skilled preacher. Their previous pastor's inability in this area had caused all the members to regard good preaching as the primary quality they were looking for in a new pastor. They found a man who regarded this area as his primary skill. They called him and all was well for a while. But then his lacks in administration, visitation, and representing the church in the community started to be the subject of much conversation. And this was so precisely because he was such a good preacher. What they had perceived as their primary lack had been filled! Inevitably secondary ones rose up to void the fill.

Inefficient. Even when there is alignment on the pastoral task, primary and secondary, stress is still a very real possibility. This is so because the pastoral task may be accomplished in a way that is unacceptable to the congregation. It may be accomplished poorly, belatedly, insensitively, begrudgingly, or just differently. A church not too far away from mine went on a search for a Bible teacher to fill their empty pulpit. They found one with an eminent reputation from another part of the country. He was called to teach the Bible and he does. This pastor teaches the Bible, book by book, chapter by chapter, verse by verse, lecturing for at least forty-five minutes every Sunday morning (more in the evenings). The worship bulletin contains his main points in outline form; the congregation is to fill in all the sub- and sub-sub-points. Attendance has declined by about fifty percent and disgruntled parishioners have even come to me to "catharse." "Well," I piped up, "if he's interesting and applies the Biblical truths to everyday living, so what if he is long and pedantic? And besides isn't that what you wanted when you called him?" "Ah," they responded, "he's deadly dull, boring and there is not one word of it that connects with my daily life! It's all just so academic. And, no. We wanted a Bible *teacher* not a *Bible* teacher."

Recourses for Transformation

Crossed energy in the area of task definition of the pastoral role can be enriching, as it starts to get at what it means to pastor and be pastored. Most folk, including pastors, can't articulate clearly and cogently their understanding of pastoring. Such a definition exists within them, but it exists at a level below clear articulation. It may have been formed in relation to the pastor of one's childhood, or at one's conversion, or at a particularly meaningful spiritual period. Parts can be—and frequently are—expressed, but the whole is located somewhere in their experience, not their expression. So stress in this area is an invitation to a ministry agenda: defining ministry for us, for now, for here.

The first step in wresting a blessing from these crossed energies is to name them. For pastors this means initially some meditation and soul searching. I remember a sermon from many years ago in which an older pastor asked some of us younger ones, "Who are you playing to? Who is the audience from whom you are seeking approval?" He went on to tell about his own playing to a seminary professor who had made a deep impression on him, so deep that years after seminary he was still doing ministry as the professor had defined it. And he went on to tell of the day he realized he needed to play to a greater audience: God. In that realization he was freed to be the pastor the people needed at that point. Each pastor plays to God, sure, but in the form of his or her own role definition. It must be so, but we needn't keep it a secret from ourselves. By consideration of the ten tasks, analysis of our past behavior, and asking trusted friends, we can come to some clarity regarding our definition of the tasks of ministry.

This process of self-awareness is important for the congregation to accomplish also. Fortunately, some tools have already been developed for us. Loren Mead ends the article "Ten Models of Pastoral Ministry"[2] with a process for using these insights with church governing boards, leaders, etc. A different process with similar outcomes is called "The Card Game," adapted by Steve Burt.[3] It goes like this: A card is made for each model. Each member of the church's governing board or group of leaders is asked to sequence the cards according to their own priority. The top three and bottom three choices of each member are shared for what they reveal about the church's perception of ministry.

The second step is to work out the implications of the learnings in step one. Several outcomes are possible here. A joyous one is that the crossed energy is trivial compared to the amount of aligned energy; with only minor adjustments the pastor and congregation can roar out of their pit stop! A less joyous one might be the realization that there is little alignment between pastor and people and that a major change in the pastor, congregation, or employment may be indicated. More typically, an adjustment or some horse trading may be the remedy. For example, the pastor might agree to develop ministry in a certain task area (one that the congregation values more than the pastor does) with the understanding that another task area, which is highly motivating to the pastor but not to the congregation, may continue with their approval, if not their active support. (That seems a pretty fair description of how I got the time to write this book!) Another outcome, an exciting one, might be the realization that a task the congregation values is not going to be accomplished by the pastor and so they rise up and take it on themselves! Yet another outcome is that both pastor and congregation are driven to ask, in prayer and Bible study and compassion for their neighbors, what is

God's definition of ministry for us, today and in the days ahead, in this place! Another outcome might be pastoral and/or congregational self-acceptance. Sometimes we put upon ourselves the trip that we have to be all things to all people, or a congregation that offers something for everyone. How much better to realize that there are several different ways to fulfill God's calling and that God's will is to be who God made and called us to be!

Resources for Further Study

Burt, Steve, *Activating Leadership in the Small Church*, Valley Forge: Judson Press, 1988.

Clark, Margaret Fletcher, "Ten Models of Ordained Ministry," *Action Information,* vol. ix, no. 5 (Nov.-Dec. 1983).

Fletcher, John C., *Religious Authenticity in the Clergy,* Bethesda, MD: The Alban Institute, 1975.

The Pastoral Role as Function

Forces at Work

The pastoral role contains many tasks as we have seen. But is there a more unified theme? Is there a central function that the pastoral role is essentially about? Yes! Let us consider what it is.

I chatted with the young pastor, a friend of mine from many years ago. How was his pastoring going? He answered that I wouldn't believe how spiritually dead the church was when he got there. But he'd finally gotten some new folks interested in sharing their faith, although he was getting a lot of grief from some of the older, unspiritual members. So there was some hope for the church, but he couldn't understand how the old guard could possibly claim to be Christians when they were so obviously unspiritual. As we talked further, I realized that he had defined "spiritual" to mean a particular style of extraverted pietism. I parted from our meeting with a vague sense of disquiet. Two weeks later I heard through a mutual friend that my spiritual friend had been asked to resign his pastorate, proving, of course, that the church was as unspiritual as he thought them to be! In one sense he was a casualty of his own pastoral role definition! He had considered it his function as pastor to spiritualize the recalcitrant. Maybe a deeper understanding of his function in the pastoral role would have proven to be more helpful all around.

As a frequent speaker at church conferences and pastors' retreats and workshops, I meet literally hundreds of pastors each year. As I talk with them, I am intrigued by their varied understandings of the role of pastor. Some talk about their responsiveness to their members needs and their continuous ability to organize activities that match the perceived needs of their parishioners. Ah, to cruise with such competent program directors on the good ship Christianity! Others talk about their great counselling load. And when I ask them if the burdens of their people don't weigh on their heart, they answer "Oh, no! It is not me with whom they are sharing their troubles; it is my pastoral counsellor role, which I leave at the church office when I go home at 5:30." (Actually said!) Others speak of their administrative skill. Others of their golf game. Others of battles with the county government. Others of their baptismal rate!

All of this leaves me feeling like the little boy who has just seen the emperor go by in his underwear! I want to cry out, Wait a minute! All of those things are about pastoring (with the possible exception of golf), but they are not pastoring. Pastoring is what its name says it is: shepherding. Caring for the flock. Pastoring is like being a rabbi in a ghetto or the chief of a tribe. It is about the "management" of persons and interpersonal relations in such a way that the whole moves toward greater spiritual health. This pastoring is political, but on a face-to-face basis. It is psychological, but in a contextual way. It is sociological, but in a personal way. It is mythological, motivational, and ecological. It is exciting and demanding, plodding and exhilarating. And it is hard to talk about. This is so because we don't have a ready vocabulary for chief-like leading. And because so few pastors seem to get it or see it as their calling and value it.

Let me give you a verbal picture. It comes from the book *Lobster Gangs*[4] and it helped me get a quick handle on interpersonal management or chief leadership. The book is a sociological study of lobster fishing off the coast of Maine, and is grounded in the author's own experience lobstering there. This story is set in a village of 250 persons, 30 of them lobstermen. These lobstermen arranged themselves into two gangs, with a 55-year-old man as the "King" of one of the gangs.

> The king's style of power is authoritarian. He has the capacity to bully other fishermen or the cooperative manager and to discipline them for real or imagined violations of norms. Their defense of the gang's fishing territory is known to be effective, if brutal. In the words of one fisherman, "They ain't always popular, but they are hard workers and have done a lot of the dirty work."

The King and his gang are used to getting their way, but their way is seen to benefit all in the village by the profitable management of the cooperative and the rigorous defense of the village's lobster "territory."

> The other leader in town is the patriarch of the largest family. "Uncle George" is a wise man, well liked by most of the people in the community. In his heyday, he was a very good lobsterman. To talk to him is to talk to a wise grandfather who can converse intelligently on virtually any subject. He is incredibly shrewd and knows every idiosyncrasy of his home town and the folk who live there. Although he usually speaks softly, he can be forceful when the occasion arises. He is one of the very few men who can stand up to the king. Fishermen often come to him when they need to talk things over, and he is inevitably the person to whom they turn when disputes arise.[6]

In the village and among the lobstermen, the King and Uncle George have different roles to play. The King is a mover and a shaker, often creating tension along the way. Uncle George is a peacemaker, the one who can find the balance point again.

> The King and Uncle George are selected by members of the harbor gangs for different purposes. One man explained that when he needs help getting something done, he goes to the king; when he needs help "getting some damage undone," he goes to Uncle George. The young manager of the cooperative said, "If you disagree with the king, you go to Uncle George." On several occasions George worked some magic for him to overturn the king's decision.[7]

Now back to pastoring. The members of a church play many dynamic roles in the life of their congregation. It is the pastoral function to know these roles *and* the rules by which they are played. Many pastors find themselves in the position of the co-op manager. Good leadership requires a working knowledge of the King, his cronies and way of operating; and of Uncle George, who he is, where he is, and when and how to call on him, if the congregation is to both move forward and stay in harmony. So the main function of the pastoral role is this kind of chief-like leadership.

Sources of Stress

Like every tribe, every congregation needs a chief or at least a council of elders. Stress arises when this need is not being met or one who has not paid his dues presumes to be chief. My friend thought his seminary bills were the dues he had to pay to pastor in a local church. Not so! Those payments are just the entry fee for paying one's dues of credibility in the local church. My friend was blindsided–and fired–just as he thought he was making spiritual progress. It was a classic case of crossed energy. He viewed his role as spiritualizer of the congregation. They wanted to live in a caring network of interpersonal relationships. They viewed his role as nurturer, not belittler, of their life together. Both parties meant well, but with such highly crossed energy, only sparks resulted.

Recourses for Transformation

The recourse for transformation is the pastor's increasing ability to "read" a pattern in, and make sense of, the behaviors of the congregation and its members--to look for the logic. Many of us have been trained to look for only one type of logic, the logical. This is what makes straightforward sense. A direct route that moves the people and congregation closer to its goals. A left brain approach. A rational strategy. When we do not find this "logic" present, we see the organization as being patho-*logical*. These people sure put a lot of energy into getting nowhere; they must be sick. I suggest that there are two other logics that the stressed pastor can look for and learn from. The first is the psycho-*logical*. The key to understanding the behavior of an individual in the congregation may not be in its external function (how much it moves the group toward its goals), but in its internal function (the rewards the individual feels after the behavior). Homeostasis (aka, no changes allowed, staying in the comfort zone, "the old shoe" phenomenon, etc.) is psychologically rewarding to most people. If this "logic" is understood and dealt with on its own terms, the stress levels in the pastor and the congregation can be reduced. A second additional logic is the socio-*logical*. This logic recognizes the need of humans beings to be integrated into a social grouping. Many behaviors that appear pathological to the outside observer are instead sociologically valid once the group's roles and rules are understood. Attributions of "pathologic" ought to be the pastor's last recourse in the quest for the logic (roles and rules) that energizes the congregation.

Some wag claims that the world contains three types of people in varying proportion: Five percent who make things happen. Ten percent who know what's happening. And eighty-five percent who ask, "What happened?" Regarding interpersonal management, we might divide pastors into three groups: the naturals, the oblivious, and the gaining. Some people are naturally skilled at "interpersonal management." They exhibit a flair for reading people and dealing productively with where they are at. Without a thought they employ different strokes for different folks. They have a natural ability, but for that very reason they are seldom able to offer insight and instruction regarding this skill. They just do it. At the other end of the spectrum are the oblivious, those who haven't caught on that system management is an essential function for the pastor. The oblivious can make good research scientists, assembly line workers or solitaire players, but they are fatally crippled in the pastorate. The pastor has to be able to work with, in, and through people.

The third category are those who are gaining skill in interpersonal management. How does this happen? Well, my old crossing guard's advice is still hard to top: Stop, look, and listen! Pastors have to stop with their agenda. It has been truly said that you don't learn very much with your mouth open. As long as we are busy directing the congregation (no matter how spiritually worthy our energy is), we are not learning from them. Look. Observe what is happening. Did you notice that deacon X only comes to the meetings if deacon Y is there and if deacon Z isn't. What does this tell you? It might be very instructive to sit on the front steps of the church on Sunday morning and see who arrives with whom, when they arrive, and where they park. Are decisions routinely delayed a month? It might be wise to look at the communication patterns between meetings–someone not on the board has more authority than those on the board! Listen. Who says what to whom? Who grabs more than their share of "air time"? For whom do others always hush up to listen? What do people say about others in their presence? In their absence? Listen for things not said, nonverbal clues, and indirect communication.

The learnings from the Stop, Look, and Listen enterprise will form a script of the roles and rules that are the current "story" of the congregation. This story is constantly evolving and can be rewritten or at least edited! And that is a major part of the pastoral task. But it is essential to read the story, to know the roles and rules, before one can possibly know *how* to begin the rewriting!

Resources for Further Study

Acheson, James M., *The Lobster Gangs of Maine*, Hanover, NH: University Press of New England, 1988.

Auel, Jean, *The Clan of the Cave Bear*, New York: Bantam Books, 1980. See especially pp. 135-138 for an illustration of how the shepherding role can lead to a major cultural change.

Pappas, Anthony G., *Entering the World of the Small Church: A Guide for Leaders*, Washington, DC: The Alban Institute, 1988.

Pappas, Anthony G., "Small Church Pastor: Tourist, Missionary or Anthropologist," *The Five Stones*, Vol. 5, No. 2 (Spring, 1987), 7-9.

"Seeds of Renewal" is a congregational renewal program that highlights this role of pastoral leadership. More information, including how to obtain a manual exploring this topic in depth, is available from Rev. David Laubach, Division of Congregational Ministry, American Baptist Churches/USA, PO Box 851, Valley Forge, PA 19482-0851.

The Symbolic Pastoral Role

Forces at Work

Another level at which the pastor plays a role for the congregation is the symbolic. The pastor is assigned a role that meets the psycho-social needs of the members of the congregation or the congregation as a whole. An individual pastor may or may not be well suited to play the symbolic role assigned to him or her. However, it would be a mistake to take this assignment too personally or too lightly. It arises out of the psycho-functioning of the congregation. It is an expression of the religio-symbolic needs of the congregation. Of course, the pastor may set up or collude with this force, too. Stress occurs when the pastor is baffled or angered by this mythic assignment. Pathology is present when the pastor accepts (or even asks for) a symbolic role that preserves the status quo, at a level less than God's intention.

What is this symbolic-mythic role? It is akin to the roles set up in dysfunctional families, such as *the scapegoat.* We will look at family systems dynamics a bit more in the next chapter. This is more "psycho-mythic systems dynamics" for it concerns the way people handle their meaning world (more than their relational world, acknowledging that there cannot be a clear distinction). When persons experience psycho-spiritual needs at an unconscious level, they often will "meet" those needs in a symbolic manner. This allows them the comfort of not having to raise these needs into consciousness and deal with them, their implications and the changes necessary for healthy fulfillment. If, however, this energy builds up and it can be discharged on a lightning rod, it will be. This permits the lightning rod to be "blamed" and the sources of the energy to remain unexamined. Unfortunately for the pastor, the pastoral role is well suited to function as a lightning rod because of all the spiritual, mythological, superstitious, magical, moral, and superego baggage that has become attached to it over the millenia. Of course, many psycho-spiritual roles cannot be brought fully into consciousness because by their very nature they transcend cognitive, rational thought. Thus we may theologize about the priest's role, but when one functions as a priest for another the investment of meaning will always be deeper than any explicit articulation. This is functionally healthy, and as it should be.

There are many positive psycho-spiritual roles, and many roles that can be either positive or negative. But for our purposes—transforming stress— we will consider a number of primarily negative psycho-spiritual roles operative in specific congregations. Let's look at some of these roles.

The Sinless One. At first glance it may seem a compliment for the pastor to be seen as so like unto Christ as to be (nearly) sinless. But the script that attaches to this role shows it to be nothing more than a con. The unwritten rule of this role is that the pastor must live a morally exemplary life. As a model for the congregation? Oh, no! Rather, a vicarious substitute for the congregation! The congregation participates in righteousness through the pastor, and so is absolved from direct acquisition. Should the pastor sin and become like the congregation, their salvation ceases, and all hell breaks out. But until then, the congregation will "sin all the more that grace may abound"—in the pastor. This role and the double standard it needs to continue to exist make no sense. Still it functions to preserve a less than healthy status quo. That is why much energy is invested in its maintenance, and much stress will result in the pastor who crosses it.

The Kicked Dog. This role is becoming increasingly popular and with it, howling and whimpering are heard across the land. We live in a society in which fewer and fewer things are immediately controllable at the local level. Life-impacting decisions are made far away and impersonal, uninfluenceable forces flip people's lives around like rowboats in a storm. Of course, when things are calm and the tide is rising, this doesn't seem like such a problem. But let a recession hit and the pain increases, often to the breaking point. In areas of shrinking population and income, and increasing bankruptcies, suicides, and crime, frustration can mount to intolerable levels and the need to control something, anything, becomes acute. With jobs insecure, incomes falling, teenagers rebelling, and spouses becoming liberated, there is one thing that can still be controlled: the pastor! The forced termination of the pastor, unnecessary paycuts, making life miserable for the pastor, relentless criticism of his or her family are all (pathologically) cathartic for some unhealthy congregations and very stressful for the pastor.

The Holy Garbageman. This role arises out of a sense of guilt about not doing enough for the pastor (or the church) while at the same time enjoying a consumptive lifestyle. Fred Craddock tells a story of a young pastor and his wife who answered the doorbell at the manse one day to find a leading couple of the church. They didn't have time to come in, but they went on about how much they appreciated the pastor's self - sacrificing work for the Lord in their midst and how they wished they could do more for him. So they decided that as they just had purchased a 31" color TV console and hadn't any further use for their old 13" black and white, which only got one channel anyway, why, they would just give it to the deserving pastoral family. "And besides giving it to you saves us a trip to the dump." The pastor all but choked in saying the Thank You they were obviously awaiting. The couple drove away feeling generous, ecological, considerate, charitable, and self-satisfied. Little did they realize how pitiable and naked and blind and wretched they really were. Could the stress the pastor experienced in that encounter have energized their conversion?

The Saint. A saint is one who is attributed to be so other worldly as to be beyond the everyday pushes and pulls of earthly life. The Saint also comes in other guises as the Holy Mother or the Reverend or in an active version as the Crusader, etc. I remember the absolute bewilderment on the faces of some older teens in town when I announced that my wife was pregnant with our first child. I suppose it was some vestigal idea of clerical celibacy that fed their confusion. For a moment I considered it a compliment that they thought I could live in such close proximity to such a beautiful woman as Cindy and have the self control never to touch her. But then I realized that they must take me for some kind of Platonic fool. Well, we've had another child since; that'll show 'em! The function of this attribution of transhuman living is distancing. If I conceive of the pastor as a qualitatively different person from myself, then I can insulate myself from his or her moral appeal. "Pastor, that works for you because you are not like me, you don't know what I'm going through. Sure you have your temptations and your crosses to bear, but they are not like mine! Mine are real." And so this role comes close to being a sad version of the Sinless One. Another version is the Fragile One, the pastor who couldn't bear to know what goes on in the real world and so must be protected from reality by a conspiracy of silence from the congregation.

The Puppet. This is the "positive" version of the Kicked Dog. Because of some supposed superiority—in years, in wisdom, in holding the purse strings, etc.—one or more congregants attempt to guide, direct, or command the pastor. For pastors with victimization tendencies this is a very seductive role. If things go well some glory can be claimed. If not, then the pastor can say, "It's all Mr. Bossman's fault; I never thought that was a good idea." For the rest it can be frustrating and stressful. A more healthy version has the congregants playing roles such as elder or elderstatesman or cabinet member, which allow energies to align or be dealt with head on.

Of course, there are thousands of other symbolic roles, but this should be enough to identify the species.

Sources of Stress

The immediate source of stress lies in the capacity of these roles to blindside an unsuspecting pastor. These are symbolic roles and meet needs that are below the consciousness of the congregation. They represent solutions that are "acted out," not "worked out." If the pastor is not into playing this particular game (which is often a healthy place to be), crossing of energies or stress will result. The pastor is likely to feel angry, frustrated, confused, resentful, or a number of other dynamic indicators. The pastor may in fact have his or her own set of symbolic roles he or she wishes to foist on the congregation, which may be as unwilling to play them out as the pastor is unwilling to play out theirs. This results in one or more layers of stress. Let me reiterate that stress in relation to these negative symbolic roles is healthy! At least it is a healthy start. These negative symbolic roles are quick and cheap fixes, not solutions. Yet they connect to real issues. So stress here is like a fever. It indicates a sickness that, if dealt with, may be healed.

Recourses for Transformation

Sadly, the first recourse involves the recognition that some pathologies are beyond our healing. Even Jesus did not heal all who were sick, only those who were willing to be healed. Symbolic roles sometimes touch areas that are deep within the soul, areas that the individual has invested much energy in keeping from the surface, areas that, though diseased, have become essential to that persons identity and can only be healed by a true metanoia (repentance). A healthy pastor can invite such a transformation, but cannot make it happen. A healthy pastor accepts this limitation as reality and makes assessments for ministry with the congregation in light of it.

Let me tell you a less than happy story from my pastoring. When I arrived on Block Island, I inherited, as chairman of the Trustee Board, an avowed, articulate, and proselytizing atheist! Virtually all of my pastoral visits turned into debates on the nonreasonableness of Christianity—at his insistence. (I've found there is a certain personality in the church, many times a sincere and deep Christian, who likes to go a few rounds with the pastor on whatever point of theology they think they can beat up on. Because I am never horrified by this, actually I enjoy the debate and like to discern whether their thinking is ahead, behind, parallel, or askew to mine, I invest great intellectual and little emotional energy in the enterprise. This posture on my part seems to take all the fun out of it for them and they soon quit the game. This man, however, had no intention of quitting.) As with debating, so with running the church; he was used to the upper hand. He did much good with it, to be sure, but after a while his constricted view of Christianity came to hamstring the church through the budgeting process that was a trustees' responsibility. As long as he and I agreed on a course of action or a posture for the church, he kept the symbolic role of puppeteer and the pastoral role of puppet in place. But when I disagreed, much energy was crossed in the conflict. He was offered many opportunities to relinquish the puppeteer role (as he offered me many opportunities to retain the puppet role!). But the puppeteer role was too close to his essential identity to relinquish for the role of Christ's disciple! Later his daughter, continuing to think in his puppeteer terms, accused me of "forcing him out of the church." My own assessment was that he took his marbles and went home when he couldn't find enough people to play his game with him. Whatever, there was no transformation and that was painful and sad.

A second and happier recourse is based on the assumption (hope, wishful thinking) that sincere Christians do not want to be the victim of forces of which they have no awareness. If sincere Christians are going to "act out," it will be an acting out of Christ's love, not an acting out of negative unconscious symbolic roles. So a recourse for transformation invites the unconscious energies to come forward and identify themselves. This is dangerous and even holy ground and should not be attempted in a mean or cavalier spirit. It might be enough to identify the role and the discomfort it causes the pastor. "I appreciate the concern toward me you are showing in offering this old TV. However, when you give me something that is unworthy of your continued use, I feel that I might fall into that same category—unworthy. I wonder what is really being said in this gift."

I seldom have the courage or quick wits to be so opportunistic in ministry. I tend to be more generalizing and deliberate. Sermons, Bible study, board and business meetings offer contexts of a more plodding type. A deacons meeting/retreat game on symbolic roles could be very revealing. "Name that Role!" Descriptions, icons, roles of previous pastors, roles that pastors put on congregations, etc, could be elements of such a game.

Sometimes just bringing unconscious forces into the light of day robs them of their power. Group awareness of these roles can initiate a process of ongoing monitoring and naming which, if done in a spirit of love and support, can move the congregation's life toward greater health.

Jesus told a parable of the expulsion of seven devils. What will now fill our souls? Maybe, the naming of our symbolic roles will motivate a Bible or church polity/history study about finding healthy roles or positive ways to meet the needs that energize the roles or bring about a healing of the hurt that formed the roles in the past.

Again we point to the frame, name, and tame process. Frame the roles by explaining/describing them and their energy. Name the roles that are operative in us as individuals and as a congregation. Tame the energy behind the roles for healthy functioning and moving closer to God's will.

Resources for Further Study

See parallels in Family Systems Dynamics in Edwin Friedman, *Generation to Generation*, New York: The Guilford Press, 1985.

Conclusion

Developing clarity, breadth, and health in the pastoral roles that are held
by the congregation and the pastor will go a long way toward a dynamic
congregation and a eustressed pastor. Now we move on to consider
dynamics based on the congregation as a social system.

CHAPTER 5

Stress in Congregational Dynamics

Introduction

The next arena is the corporate life of the local congregation. We have been moving in ever widening circles of exploration, from the soul of the pastor, to the potentials and pitfalls of interpersonal relationships, to the role definition of "pastor." Now we consider the dynamics inherent in the systemic life of the congregation as a living, social organism. Five aspects are presented: patterns of power and communication, size-related dynamics, congregational culture, the life cycle of the congregation, and family systems.

Patterns of Power and Communication

Forces at Work

Life merrily plunks along in that broad gray area between total chaos and absolute certainty. Yet in the midst of all the pieces of life the wise soul (and pastor) will discern certain operative patterns. These patterns are not inviolable, but they do serve to make sense of a large portion of the surrounding behavior.

In the congregation there are patterns of power—who makes decisions in specific circumstances—and patterns of parlance—who talks to who about what and when. While configurations of authority and patterns of communication are not identical, they are similar enough to be

treated the same for our purposes. Knowledge is power or close enough
for us.

So what patterns of power and parlance are exhibited in our congregations? There are four patterns. One or a hybrid is operative in most congregations. The four patterns I have dubbed, for mnemonic purposes,
the Washer, the Wedge, the Wheel, and the Web. Let us examine each
briefly.

The Washer, as those of us who shrink in terror from the printing on the
package "Some assembly required" know, refers to a metallic disk with a
hole in the middle. In some congregations the pastor feels like the hole
in the middle of the washer. He or she is located in the center of things
—worship, weddings, funerals—but somehow things happen at the periphery and the pastor only catches on belatedly, if at all. The congregation has learned often through long and sometimes bitter experience to
function independently. Maybe a succession of supply or student pastors, maybe a very hurtful experience with the previous pastor, or maybe
social or demographic factors have allowed or required the congregation
to function to the exclusion of the pastor. The pastor is hired as a func-
tionary and is out of the power-communication loop. (See the section
on size dynamics page 82.) The strength of the Washer pattern lies in its
capacity to endure against formidable odds and the high level of ownership in the congregation itself. Weaknesses include the low level of pastoral impact possible, and the inability to attract or keep a quality pastor
in such an unrewarding structure.

The Wedge represents the opposite configuration of communication and
power. The Wedge is like an pyramidal organization in which power
and "truth" flow down from the top. The pastor in the Wedge is all
powerful. PreVatican II Catholic theology of the church and cults such
as David Koresh's illustrate the Wedge pattern of power and communication. Advantages of the Wedge are revealed in times of crisis allowing
for quick and unified response. And in the short run the Wedge is quite
efficient. Weaknesses lie in the inexorable disenfranchisement of
everyone in the organization who isn't in or near the point, and in the
increasingly poor quality of decisions made by the point position as
feedback dies before it reaches the top.

The Wheel configuration places the pastor at the hub with the laity embodying the surrounding circle. Their communication and decision making as the spokes connecting the two. Communication can flow around the perimeter or to and through the hub. The pastor in the Wheel is truly in the center of things (as contrasted to the Washer) and often feels that he or she is carrying a heavy load, but a highly satisfying one. Advantages of this pattern include high pastoral reward, centralized knowledge, and experience allowing for coordinated action. Disadvantages include the plateauing of congregational relationships and the bottleneck effect of running most everything through the pastor.

The Web is similar to the Wheel but instead of one central position, there are many. Communication flows from any point to virtually any other point. Decisions may be made in diverse places depending on expertise, experience, and interest. The Web is an active matrix of relationships, information processing, ownership, and decision making. The advantages of the Web include high ownership among the members, high quality decisions made at the points of impact, and a dynamism in the whole organization. Disadvantages include the high costs of coordination, and slowness to galvanize in times of crisis.

Sources of Stress

The basic source of stress in communication and authority patterns occurs when the pastor has one form in mind and the congregation is used to operating in another. The result is a classic case of stress as crossed expectations. The pastor may see himself as the God-appointed point in the congregational Wedge. Maybe he grew up in a church of this type or has just moved from a church that was comfortable receiving unilateral marching orders, or maybe he has greater than normal power needs. The congregation, on the other hand, may be very content with a Wheel pattern. Experience crosses with expectations. Stress results. Of course, it could be the other way, too. A dependent congregation may be looking to be told what to do. A Wheel or Web pastor will be just as stressed, but this time in the opposite direction. And it doesn't matter to stress whether the crossed expectations are closer (e.g., Wheel to Web) or farther apart (e.g., Wheel to Washer). I have determined that part of

my pastoral ministry at this period in the life of our congregation on
Block Island is to encourage the move from Wheel to Web patterns. In
so doing I have been reprimanded, have watched people walk away
dazed, and overheard others replay my Web script as if I were speaking
Chinese. It's fun; it's challenging; and it's Stress!

Another aspect of stress results when initially the patterns seem harmonious. A Washer congregation gets a Washer pastor, etc. Expectations and experience are aligned. No stress. At least not at first. But
eventually the inherent weakness of each pattern will surface. People
will wonder why things aren't working as well as they should. A Wedge
pastor will start out leading a happy band toward the promised land, only
to find that the people aren't listening so well anymore. A Web pastor
may have many happy years pastoring a Web congregation, but let a
crisis occur and people start to expect situationally appropriate leadership. Oops! Stress again.

A third form of stress occurs in the deliberate attempt to meddle with
existing patterns. In this instance the stress is not generated by the surprise of crossed expectations, but by the energy expended to stay in our
comfort zones. This task often feels Promethean. Pastoral stress may
occur in the energy crossed between the necessity of changing patterns
(internal) and the desire to do "real" ministry (outreach). More on this
when we consider congregational culture.

Recourses for Transformation

Have I introduced you to Pappas's First Law of Congregational Dynamics? It is not as famous as Murphy's Law, but it describes a truth with
the same feeling tone. It is: Patterns Persist. Corollary A is Patterns
Resist any an attempt to mess with the First Law. So Patterns Persist and
Resist, and anyone who would change them would be well advised to
count the cost. Sometimes it is enough to recognize the different patterns between the pastor and the congregation. An easy going congregation and pastor might well come to chuckle over the instances of crossed
energy resulting from these patterns.

When a pastor determines that a change in pattern is consistent with
God's will for the church, then certain steps may prove effective. Try to
raise the pattern to consciousness. Ask a fish about the water it lives and

moves and has its being in and it will just look at you with big uncom-
prehending eyes. The fish has an excuse, but you'll get the same response (or worse) from church members if you cross habitual patterns
without first helping members to identify them. This needn't be overly
threatening. "You know, in the church I grew up in, the pastor made all
the big decisions. We carried them out. I guess I went into the ministry
with that idea. But I find you all rather independent. In some ways I like
that. But I hope you'll be patient with me as I adjust to you. And I hope
you can meet me in the middle, too."

Bring the key leadership in on your commitment to change patterns.
The whole congregation may not grasp or care about the change, but the
key leaders are crucial to effecting change. If they won't support movement, it might be well advised to regroup.

Demonstrate and model the new pattern. Accept that it will be dis-
sonant with the congregration's expectations and develop a thick skin.
Allow love to always be present whatever pattern you work out of.
Accept that a hybrid may be a reasonable goal for the given time frame.
Try to reward new behaviors and affirm those living them.

Resources for Further Study

Hersey, Paul and Kenneth H. Blanchard, *Management of Organizational
Behavior: Utilizing Human Resources*, Englewood Cliffs, NJ: Prentice
Hall, 1977. This book proposes a more detailed model for describing
and prescribing leadership behaviors.

Stevens, R. Paul and Phil Collins, *The Equipping Pastor: A Systems
Approach to Congregational Leadership*, Washington, DC: The Alban
Institute, 1993.

Size-Related Dynamics

Forces at Work

Quantity shapes quality. The nature of something depends on its size. Last night I attended Block Island's town financial meeting. It was democracy at work. Everyone who wanted to attended, spoke, and voted. Presidents talk about holding national town meetings, but it's just talk. Two hundred and fifty million people can't make democracy work. Such a large population is stuck with representational federalism. Not necessarily bad, but not democracy either. Size has determined form and function.

This is an organizational truth that is often overlooked in our congregations and in our training for the pastorate. Size is a major determining factor of the nature of congregational dynamics and the functioning of the pastor. I relearned this truth when I was invited by the Midwest Commission on the Ministry of the American Baptist Churches USA to do some research on bivocational pastors, their tasks, and training. I interviewed over a dozen pastors in four states—a small sampling, but with replicable results. The way pastors described their tasks fell into four categories. Here is a representative sampling:

1. "I preach the first and third Sunday morning of each month. I get $35 a week. Also, an occasional wedding or funeral . . . Conflict? No, not in the two years I've been there." (West Virginia bivocational pastor)

2. "I love these people. That's why I'm in it. It's sure not for the big bucks! . . . .I made the motion (to fund an outreach youth ministry) and my wife seconded it. I was gonna make sure we did it." (West Virginia bivocational pastor)

3. "Right after Easter, I'm going to a key lay person and get him to head up a prayer chain. He can get together some people in the church, and he can organize it. Also, I'm going to head up visitation . . . As I pass off these responsibilities, I can work on the next issue." (West Virginia bivocational pastor)

4. "We are what's left of a large church before all their children left this suburb. We are an older congregation and someday we will die . . . In the meantime, I am building up my counselling practice." (Chicago area bivocational pastor)

As I spoke further with the pastors who fall into each of these categories, I came to realize that the congregations they pastored also fell into four categories, distinguished by size and dynamics.

Congregation A usually had fewer than forty at worship. Its members identified strongly with the church due to family connection or long-term residency. The congregation handled their witness and service, Christian education and maintenance needs, at least at a level acceptable to their own membership. Their fellowship was tight and significant. Their primary need is to have worship led, sermons preached, and ceremonies conducted. This is the "Family Chapel" type and is pastored by a "Preacher" (cf quotation 1 page 82).

Congregation B usually has forty to eighty at worship and often a greater number of people in the "next circle" too. Members identified significantly with the church, but not totally. Transition on the membership rolls is small but definite. The congregation operates out of tradition but is open to pastoral guidance. Their primary need is to be nurtured, held together, and affirmed. Let's call this type "Personal Church" and its leader a "Pastor" (cf quotation 2 page 82).

Congregation C usually has 80-120 at worship. It experiences significant elements of transition in both membership and church activities. Its culture and social life are maintained by leadership acts, as much as by tradition and inertia. Its life needs to be administered. This congregation has an energizing sense of potency relative to its environment. This is the "Transitional Church" and requires a "Minister" (cf quotation 3 page 82).

Congregation D is variable in number, but always less than the Golden Days. It expects a professional level of performance from its minister, whose educational level is above average. This congregation often exhibits a survival mentality reinforced by an eroded membership and financial base. This is the "Institutional Remnant" church and is served by a "Reverend" (cf quotation 4 above).

If we composed a chart of these four types of pastors and their four congregational types, it might look like this:

Church	Clergy	Skills	Functions
Chapel	Preacher	Technical	Lead worship, preach, ceremonial
Personal	Pastor	Personal	Above, plus care for members and nurture body life
Transitional	Minister	Administrative	Above, plus organize internal life and ministry beyond the congregation
Remnant	Reverend	Professional	Preaching, counselling; pastor represents congregation to denominational and outside world, maintaining forms of earlier ministries with reduced content

Interestingly, my results replicated the findings of others. Arlin Rothauge[1] divides congregations into four size categories, each with different qualities and characteristics. The Family Church (up to 50 members) operates informally as a single cell. The Pastoral Church (50-150 members) requires a more differentiated leadership and multiple cells revolving around the pastor. The Program Church (150-350 members) operates with a staff that facilitates the laity's gifts and sees its success in the quality and quantity of its activities. The Corporate Church (300+ members) is more complex and diverse with bureaucratic divisions and procedures.

Lyle Schaller[2] also places churches in categories by size. The fewer than 35-member church is like a cat, independent and resilient. The 35-100 member church is like a collie, affectionate and loyal towards its master. The 100-175 member church is like a garden, requiring much cultivation but yielding a good harvest. The 175-225 member church is like a house, unique, livable, but in constant need of repair and even remodeling, etc. Schaller sums it all up: One size does NOT fit all!

The most vivid size-related description was shared over dinner one night by Doug Walrath: "New church? It's no secret how to grow a large church. You start with a people-person pastor who gathers some very loving people around him or her. When the group gets to a plateau, you take him out and shoot him and put in a program pastor. As he gets things buzzing and whirring and the church grows to its next plateau, you take him out and shoot him, and bring in an administrator type pastor. It'll work, as long as you don't mind having dead bodies around."

Sources of Tension

To use pejorative language that unabashedly proclaims my bias, the sources of tension related to size dynamics are 1) ignorance, 2) arrogance, and 3) homeostasis.

Ignorance

In my book *Entering the World of the Small Church*,[3] I recount my journey into the bewildering world of size dynamics. I had naively and inaccurately assumed that small and large were simply quantitatively different points on a single, qualitative spectrum of social organizations. I was in for a rude awakening and a lot of growth (after a comparable amount of pain!). The pastor who expects a small church to operate like a business, and the pastor who expects a large church to operate like a tribe are in for large doses of stress.

In the small church things are done personally, the group is oriented toward the past, tradition is the main method of operation, and much energy is expended to keep the social fabric from unravelling. The small church knows itself in its "being" and desires a pastor with strong relational abilities. These key elements indicate that the small church operates out of a tribal paradigm.

In contrast the mid-sized church operates more out of a business paradigm. Their focus is on doing and their pastor should be capable of administering goodly amounts of activities. They know themselves in their programming; they look less to the past, more to the future, but clearly to the present; they are "intentional" in all they do and don't care if the softball team ever fellowships with the chancel choir.

The large church is a quantum jump beyond the mid-sized church. They operate out of a bureaucratic paradigm and install a pastor with CEO skills. Their world is filled with "ministries" (e.g., departments, bureaus); they are proactive and future-oriented and compartmentalized.

Of course, there are undoubtedly as many hybrid churches as pure types, size-anomalous churches (e.g., a ghetto ethnic church can exhibit tribal characteristics even when its members number in the many hundreds), and any "real" church is always more than these categories paint it to be. Nevertheless, when most seminary graduates come out of mid- and large-sized suburban churches and go immediately to pastor small, rural or urban churches, we have in place a formula for massive stress. Just *knowing* that quantity shapes quality can be a lifesaver.

Arrogance
David Ray[4] argues that American society has a built-in bias toward bigness. He calls this sizism. This attitude is expressed in the slogan "Bigger is Better." And perforce smaller stinks! In Christ's church we have naively and sinfully baptized this value of society and read it back into the scriptures. So growing churches are successful and large churches are good; and implicitly shrinking churches and small churches are pathological.[5]

Yes, churches should grow, but growth is more than numbers.[6] It is also faithfulness, ministry, and personal, familial, and corporate health and maturity. I believe that God is retooling the church[7] and that it will be a leaner, meaner version that emerges. Current definitions of success will, de facto, be scrapped! I offer two thoughts to help counter the arrogance of sizism: 1) Nothing fails like success (e.g., the Constantinian church grew by leaps and bounds, yet most church historians cannot point to a larger spiritual disaster), and 2) God calls us, not to success necessarily, but always to faithfulness.

Homeostasis
Stasis is the Greek word meaning to stand, stand firm, often interpreted to stand still, be static. Homeostasis refers to the dynamic quality of a system to absorb a change and return to its original state. Congregations are homeostatic organizations. If a certain size dynamic is written into

the "DNA" (determinative vision) of the congregation, it will maintain itself in that size range, or the qualitative functioning of that size range, despite many different experiences and environmental and organizational changes. Thus a pastor with the expectation of church growth, even when armed with the verbal blessings of the congregation, will often find him or herself experiencing a spike or dynamic plateau in membership (people changing but the totals remaining within a certain range). Stress is often the result of this crossing of pastoral expectation with the experience of congregational homeostasis. [8]

Pastors also have certain giftedness that suits them for certain size-related organizational characteristics. Pastors will undergo stress if they expect congregational growth and work hard toward that end, but experience size stasis unless they realize that their own giftedness and competence are often the homeostatic energy that maintains the congregation at that size! For example, unless a "Personal Pastor" of a small church gives up the satisfaction of relationships for the duties and functions of the "Administrative Minister," his or her congregation is unlikely to move to midsize.

Should a congregation change in size (and therefore size-related character), the original membership often feels alienation, not victory and joy. Thus the original members of a small church, which with dynamic pastoral leadership breaks into the program church level, will feel as though they are on the outside looking in, wondering who all these new people are, and not how, but even if they fit in any more. The pastor who expects elation from these members only to get alienation will experience stress. [9]

Recourses for Transformation

Learn

There is no reason nowadays why we pastors and church leaders cannot be size-dynamic savvy. There is a literature, in print and (relatively) cheap. Seminaries offer courses (even if the implications do not affect the curriculum much). And people like myself stump the country, proclaiming this Gospel. (Actually, one of the soul-satisfactions God has graced me with is the feedback from struggling pastors on how helpful size dynamic insights have been for their pastoring and personal well-being, not to mention the congregation's!)

Leave

Leave what? Leave behind ignorance and arrogance, yes. But also,
often, just plain leave. I remember a letter I received about ten years ago
from a young pastor. We had corresponded about the qualities, world
view, and methods of operating of small churches. The letter went on
and on about the helpfulness of these insights. Then the final paragraph
announced his resignation from the church, as he realized that he was
not gifted for that type of ministry! I was crushed! Unwittingly I had
pushed a person out the door of small church ministry. I had terrifying
visions of Jesus, the millstone, the sea, and me! But soon I regrouped.
God has equipped different people to pastor differently, congregations to
operate better in one organizational context than another. One aspect of
good ministry is knowing your context and serving God faithfully there.
Some pastors can serve God equally well in small, large, and mid-sized
congregations. But these are rare birds. Most of us, even the very best
of us, work best in one context.[10] If, after learning, you determine that
your stress is due to the square peg/round hole phenomenon, leave. Get
to where God intends you to be.

Leaven

If however you believe that God has equipped you to minister in the
congregational context in which you currently serve, then get on with
it—according to the nature of that social organism! Four distinct leadership roles fit each of the four sized congregations respectively: Ceremo-
nialist, Chief, Cruise Director, and CEO. Match your gifts/style to the
size/nature of the congregation, continue to develop the appropriate skills,
and minister. Working with the nature of the congregation is more
effective than working against it!

Level

The last recourse is to change the size level of the congregation until it
matches the gifts/role of the pastor. Thus a tribal chief pastor can let
the programs of a program-size church atrophy until the congregation
shrinks to "collie" size. Or a Cruise Director pastor can build up a
family church until it offers something for everyone. This will relieve
the stress between the pastor's preferred way of operating and the congregation, but it may invoke integrity-generated stress issues.

Resources for Further Study

American Baptist Quarterly, vol. 1x, no. 2 (June 1990). Small Church Issue.

American Baptist Quarterly, vol. xi, no. 1 (March 1992).

Burt, Steven E. and Hazel A. Roper, *Raising Small Church Esteem,* Washington, DC: The Alban Institute, 1992.

Dudley, Carl S., *Making the Small Church Effective,* Nashville: Abingdon Press, 1978.

The Five Stones - Newsletter for Small Churches, Box D2, Block Island, RI 02807.

Mead, Loren B., *More Than Numbers: The Ways Churches Grow,* Washington, DC: The Alban Institute, 1993.

Oswald, Roy M., *How to Minister Effectively in Family, Pastoral, Program and Corporate Sized Churches,* Washington, D.C.: The Alban Institute, 1991. On demand publication.

Pappas, Anthony G., *Entering the World of the Small Church: A Guide for Leaders,* Washington, DC: The Alban Institute, 1988.

Ray, David R. *Small Churches Are the Right Size,* New York: The Pilgrim Press, 1982.

Ray, David R., *The Big Small Church Handbook,* Cleveland: The Pilgrim Press, 1992.

Rothauge, Arlin J., *Sizing Up a Congregation for New Member Ministry,* New York: The Episcopal Church Center, 1983.

Schaller, Lyle E., *Looking in the Mirror: Self-Appraisal in the Local Church,* Nashville: Abingdon Press, 1984.

Congregational Culture

Forces at Work

Culture has been likened to the air we breathe. It is everywhere, necessary to life as it is experienced, and yet "invisible" to those within it.

There are many circles of culture: familial, congregational, community, and societal. Using its own vocabulary, family systems theory impacts family culture as it "solves" the recurrent problems of family life (more on this below). In the next chapter we will follow Tex Sample's three-fold analysis of societal culture. The culture of the surrounding community affects to some extent the culture of the congregation. We will focus on congregations' culture because community culture is highly variable and much written about whereas congregational culture is a novel concept to many pastors and church leaders. [References to community culture are provided in the following Resources section.]

Larry Gibbons points us to the power and invisibility of congregational culture.

> A seminary classmate shared this heartbreaking story at our class reunion. A fellowship meal was planned at church. My classmate made a special effort to see that a new family was included in the event. He watched with joy as the wife brought a beautiful strawberry pie, placed it on the dessert table, and covered it with whipped cream from a pressurized can. His joy turned to horror when a longtime church member calmly walked over, picked up the pie, then flushed it down the garbage disposal, announcing "Our church has served this farming community for a long time and we have always used real whipped cream at meals." My classmate paid more attention at future meals and, sure enough, only natural butter, bread, and whipped cream were served. This story is illustrative of the difficulty many congregations have assimilating new members. They profess a genuine desire to attract new members. But it is hard to attract new members when their pies get thrown down the garbage disposal!
>
> It is difficult to understand why congregations engage in activities that are obviously self-destructive. There is something out there that goes on in congregations, a fundamental force that accounts for

much of what happens, and can never be captured on an organizational chart or policy handbook. That invisible force is the congregation's culture. A congregation's culture is the pattern of basic behaviors that has grown out of its collective belief system. These behaviors were developed to cope with problems and they work well enough to be taught to persons entering its fellowship. The long-time member who threw the pie down the drain was doing what the culture of her congregation taught her to do. She was also saying that being a member involves much more than a formal repetition of membership. Being a full member requires some recognition of the norms expressed in the group's culture.

Because of its "invisible" quality, the culture of a congregation is hard to grasp. Here are seven "handles" to help you pull the invisible into visibility.

Some Elements of Church Culture

Gossip (talk re people)	Sick/destructive	No bonds
├───┤

Language	Unique ("foreign")	No jargon
├───┤

Congregational Story	Four stories	No story
├───┤

History	Locked in the past	Amnesia/disoriented
├───┤

Individual vs. Community	Monolithic	Atomized
├───┤

Artifacts	Identity lodged in things	No things = no identity
├───┤

Routines and Rituals	Locked in, boring	No predictability, chaos
├───┤

Rate of change	Low	High
├───┤

Let us explore the meaning of these seven dimensions. (Ways to use
them in your congregation are given in the notes.[12])

1. Gossip

Gossip is here defined as talk regarding other persons in the church.
When this talk is malicious and destructive, of course, it is evil. But
people-talk can be just as destructive of the human spirit when it is
absent! We talk about what we care about. If the other people in our
congregation don't matter enough to us to converse about them, then
Christ's love is not being realized. In a fascinating study,[13] Heilman
enumerates four kinds of congregational gossip. The simplest is knowledge that everyone is presumed to be aware of, nobody needs announce
it. Next is public knowledge. These are the common stories that are told
and retold. An individual can demonstrate that he or she is in the center
of congregational life and power if, upon another's telling of the story,
he or she can correct the ending! These stories carry the values of the
congregation; in a very real sense, the story is us! Then comes privileged
information, the coin of congregational status. And finally there is
sacred news, those items that can only be shared in special places with
special persons. In a significant sense, gossip is wealth in congregational
life, and the conversational dynamic of a congregation frequently reflects
an Oriental marketplace![14]

2. Language

If a congregation has a rich interpersonal life, it will develop a language
which is distinct. Congregations that use only the language of the dominant culture demonstrate a lack of identity, shared experience, and dynamic culture. On the other hand, congregations that live exclusively in
a language world of their own making, cut off from the resources of their
social environment, are in a vulnerable position. Congregational language, which is both distinguishable and open, is undoubtedly the most
healthy. These language clues are continuously pouring out on our ears.
Compare "Pastor Bob" to "the Rev. Dr. Smythe" or "Jeeeeeesus" to "the
good Lord," etc. The power of language to separate a congregation came
home to me one morning at our church's men's group. Our sessions are
times of fun, fellowship, and faith development. The fun is often embodied in joke telling. Over the preceding weeks a number of jokes had

become current. This particular morning an interesting phenomenon
occurred. The men started talking to each other in punchlines! Punchlines punctuated by laughter. One right after the other, six, seven, eight
in a row. The punchlines were English sentences but made no sense at
all without the context of the entire joke. A newcomer hearing this
"conversation" would have thought us all mad. But, fortunately, there
were no newcomers that morning. Of course, that would be no surprise
either. Having developed a language so specifically unique to ourselves
who could break in? I called the men on it. Now we've gone back to
telling the whole joke, boring as the prepunchline stuff is!

3. *Congregational Story*
Actually, this is not so much a congregational story—healthy congregations have many stories—as it is a congregation worldview embodied in
a story and expressed narratively. James Hopewell is our guide here.[15]
He asserts that congregations embody one of four "stories": tragedy,
comedy, irony, or romance. Simply put, tragedy avers that life is difficult, maybe even fatal, but God will win in the end. Irony takes the same
premise, but it asserts that we ought, therefore, to uphold, comfort and be
present to one another. Comedy delights in "all's well that ends well";
while romance looks to the divine to miraculously sweep us into spiritual
bliss. Hopewell helps us to relate each of these congregational story-
types to a theology: canonic, gnostic, empiric, and charismatic. For our
purposes, we can assert that a congregation is healthy if it lives in one of
these story-theology worlds while being open to inputs from the others--
all being necessary, but not sufficient to reflect the fulness of God--and
not fully healthy if it stands nowhere or tries to stand everywhere.

4. *History*
The history of the congregation is not so much what actually happened,
but what is contained in the remembered and retold stories of the congregation. These stories give meaning to the congregation's present and
guide it toward the future. A congregation's culture can be dysfunctional
if its stories become its whole world, i. e., it lives only in the past. But
congregational culture can be equally dysfunctional if it tries to live
without its stories. This amnesia will only result in disorientation. In
The Lost Mariner, Oliver Sachs[16] describes the pathos and tragedy of a
sailor who tries to make sense of his life while suffering under a condition

that allows him to remember only the preceeding five minutes. Sachs
finally concludes that this life is still worthwhile, but the reader
is left to wonder how. If this condition is pathetic for individuals, might
it be even more so for congregations? The Bible condemns Esau for
trading away his birthright. Without the blessing of his past, Esau is
cursed. What other outcome could there be? To be without a past is
not to be free, it is to be hamstrung, unable to move forward. By God's
grace we might choose to transcend our past, but thank God we have a
past from which to make that judgement!

We might look for the stories that make up a congregation's history
in four types of myths. (I am using "myths" to mean stories that explain. This type of myth conveys a congregation's mythos or meaning.)
A) *Creation Myths.* Creation myths talk about the beginning of things.
My congregation has a number of creation myths: the settling of the
island, the founding of the church, the ministry of Dr. Roberts, the arrival
of Tony Pappas. The last one is especially important to me! But it is
important to the congregation, too. To invite me, the congregation took
a big step of faith: they raised their salary to our denomination's minimum without knowing where the money was coming from! It came in
and I was paid. In the course of the last two decades I have, on occasion,
referred back to this big step of faith as we have faced new challenges
requiring new steps of faith. What was created back then is recreated
as we choose anew to be a people of faith and daring! B) *Hero myths.*
Hero myths hold up the saints of old as examples, inspiration, models,
etc., for us today. C) *Crisis myths.* These are myths which undergird our
perseverance by giving us again the message: We've had bad times
before, and look at us; we're still around to talk about them! D) *Cultural
myths.* Cultural myths explain why we do what we do the way we do it.
They often start with a version of: "Once upon a time . . ." These myths
are often revealed as one listens to the older members of the congregation.

5. *The Individual versus the Community*

A healthy congregation exhibits a culture that balances the needs and
gifts of the individual with the needs and gifts of the community. No one
point is right for all congregations in all times and places. Each must be
specifically discerned, but congregational dysfunction exists when the
individual is all or is nothing. Robert Dale tells a fascinating story about

a young couple who came to him for counselling after an unhappy church experience. They described their church as one in which there had never been any fights, disagreements, or hostilities. None? queried Dale. None, they answered. The pastor and deacons decided the church's position on each matter and the congregation followed faithfully along. Forever? asked Dale. Well, for years . . . until the day the church split! That church's culture did not allow a healthy discussion of divergent points of view. So divine diversity was denied until the truth could be no longer contained and the volcano erupted.

6. Artifacts
Every healthy culture produces artifacts that are functional and symbolic. These items accomplish what is necessary to the survival and well being of the group, and also act as containers for that which is of value to the group. These artifacts both hold and promote the congregation's culture. A culture with no artifacts is sterile and dead. A culture whose artifacts have become sacred per se and unchangeable may not be dead yet, but it will be! For a congregation's culture to be healthy it must have artifacts that are in living connection with its people and their needs. Artifacts can symbolize the presence of the saints and heroes of old and so help us to be faithful today. Artifacts can remind us of God's faithfulness in the past, as the contents of the Ark of the Covenant was meant to do for the Israelites of old. Artifacts recall to our minds the richness, creativity, faithfulness, and perseverance of the previous generations. And that is good, but when they freeze us in the past, robbing us of spiritual energy and vision, it is bad, and the temple must be cleansed of these thieves. I was told of a church that received a large bequest. A meeting room was remodelled and named after the deceased in accordance with the instructions of the will. To prevent the remaining monies from being used for other purposes in the life of the church, the deceased had specified that anything purchased from his bequest must be used in "his" room for at least six months. For a while it was the brightest and best room in the church. Everything was of top quality, new and clean. But as time went along and church income waned a bit, the cagey trustees realized that all they would have to do to keep the church provided with its necessities would be to anticipate by a half year the material needs of the church, buy them with those designated funds and store them in "his" room until six months transpired. The shrine to the memory of the deceased had

become nothing more than a closet where snowblowers, refrigerators, hymnals, and photocopiers were indiscriminately piled awaiting their release date! Every attempt to fix the life of a congregation in the things of the past can only lead to one pathology or another.

7. Routines and Rituals

When people share life together, help each other through ups and downs, share their hopes and dreams, weather storms by facing them together, and live in proximity over a long time, they develop certain routines and rites in their common life. Their routines become a shorthand for dealing with recurrent issues. Any culture that did not have these routines and rituals would chew up an inordinate amount of time in deciding and redeciding what to do, how to do it, who's to do it, and when to do it. Rituals are often a means of putting joy and awe back into behaviors that have become pretty routine. Routines and rituals are the ways healthy congregational cultures deal with the scheduling of chronos and kairos in life. It is an imperfect business to be sure, but it is a lot healthier and happier than groups who are always deciding life issues from square one (and so die off because of the high energy costs of continuously reinventing the wheel) or groups that have all of life figured out, fixed in their calendar of habit (and so die off from boredom and rigidity). Healthy congregations have routines that are functional and rituals that are fun.

8. Rate of Change

This aspect of a congregation's culture concerns its posture relative to the environment. Some congregations live in disjuncture and discontinuity from their environment. Stepping into their building, worship service, or fellowship is like stepping back into 1895 or 1795. Other congregations live on the cutting edge of society. Whatever is going on in the world is going on in their church, too. Obviously, the place of health is somewhere in the middle. Resources from the environment must be assimilated with spiritual discernment and at a pace that works. New people, ideas, and things are needed for the future well-being of the congregation, if they can be incorporated at a rate that is viable. Too slow and the congregation becomes a dinosaur. Too fast and the congregation loses its identity and even its integrity. Many well-meaning church members think that it is the environment that determines the resources that are incorporated by the congregation. But this is seldom the case. It is the congregation's culture that determines what, how much, and at what pace resources are brought into the congregation. This "invisible force" operating on the resources of the environment determines the outcome. What is often perceived as spiritual intransigence in "them" is more often spiritual "blindness" in us!

Congregational Culture

Sources of Tension

The sources of tension related to pastoring in the midst of congregation's culture are fourfold:

Landmines. Cultures have built-in mechanisms that reward behaviors that are within the norm of the culture and punish behaviors that wander too far "to the right or to the left." One foot over the lines may simply generate an uneasy silence. Two feet a mild rebuke. But wandering beyond the accepted boudaries of the congregation's culture may trigger an explosion—immediate, powerful, and violent. As witness the strawberry pie incident.

I triggered a landmine in an early sermon of mine shortly after arriving on Block Island. Preaching on Jesus' words that God could raise children to Abraham from those stones, I made an analogous assessment of what constituted true islanders. (I should have read ahead and discovered what happened to Jesus shortly after his statement!) It was an insensitive comment borne of youthful idealism and immaturity. But I grew because of it. I soon experienced the power of genealogy! The dead were not a dead issue, I learned. The genealogical lists in scripture had been irrelevant and vaguely confusing to me. No longer. Their power and potential for pain has me in awe!

Objectification and Devaluation. Culture is comfortable (more or less) because we don't have to think about it. We *like* its invisibility. To make culture evident is a stress-generating and punishable activity. The emperor's clothes were not visible, and just for that reason no adult was about to break the silence. Once as part of my doctoral work I described

a decision-making process of the deacons back to the deacons. Silence.
Scowls. Pastoral anxiety. "Did I get it wrong?" I blurted out when the
pressure had built to warning levels. "No . . . no," answered the chair.
"It was as you described it. But I don't like hearing it in so many words."
My description was not judgmental in tone. But the mere objectification
of how they operated felt judgmental and uncomfortable. They felt de-
valued. Yet the outsider or newcomer or prophet must objectify to understand and so to value. (Uncritical socialization is also possible, but no
better. More on this later.) Stress is inherent when pastors "from away"
enter the congregation's culture.

Meddling. When a pastor tries to fix something that isn't broken by the
congregation's norm, he or she will not be applauded as a savior but
derided as a meddler. A lawyer moved to Block Island a few months
ago and has taken to attending school committee meetings and at great
length apprising the committee of how they should do things better.
Finally, the chairwomen[17] announced her policy regarding his directions:
although many of his points were well taken, until it was clear he would
be a long-term resident, she wasn't about to implement his recommenda-
tions! At least she was polite about it. But meddling is not a activity
likely to engender positive forward movement. Resistance and stress are
the betting man's picks.

Inculturation, or the nontension stress. The fourth source of stress
relative to the culture of the congregation is uncritical acceptance and
acculturation over time. This produces the least explicit stress in the
pastor, but may result in infinite amounts of stress and anxiety on judgment day! Pastors are not called to baptize the culture of the congregation but to help bring it under the Lordship of Jesus Christ. How can this
be done? Let us consider some approaches.

Recources for Transformation

In a very helpful article, Larry Gibbons[18] pictures for us a process for the
change of a congregation's culture. This process is based on faithful
pastoral and lay leadership that seeks to find God's will in the unique
opportunties of a congregation.

Leadership focuses on:

1. The Situational: Critical moments in the congregation's life
2. The Theological: Envisioning a new future
3. The Managerial: Assessing new activities
4. The Mythological: Reframing the meaning of the past in light of the future
5. The Political: Mobilizing support from the congregation's members
6. The Experiential: Adaptive experimentation regarding leaders' and congregation's behaviors

Critical Moments
These are times (Kairos) when there is a unique openness to intervention in a congregation's life. A change in ministerial leadership is one of the most common critical moments. However, building projects, dramatic declines in worship attendance or financial support, the addition of new staff, and major shifts in the immediate environment can provide new openness to intervention.

Envisioning a New Future
The heart of this change process is to develop a vision of what the future should look like. Mobilization of passive persons requires their involvement in setting goals that are connected to their concerns.

Assessment
The people managing the change process must make determinations regarding the activities necessary to actualize the new vision. Assessment from this perspective involves serious analysis of congregational culture. But the focus of that analysis is on the changes necessary to move toward the new future.

Reframing
Reframing involves changing the meaning of people's interpretation of events, especially from the past, to new understandings congruent with the future vision.

Mobilizing Support
Persons must be identified who will support the desired changes. They

must be capable of making connections between the newly envisioned future and their personal desires for the congregation.

Adaptive Experimentation
This involves implementing the strategies, monitoring them, evaluating, and making adjustments when needed.

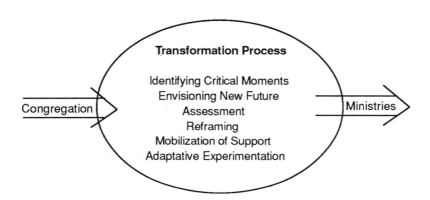

These six dimensions of cultural change in a congregation do not represent an unvarying mechanism. Rather they can be seen as a buffet of starting points for cultural transformation.

After a few years of pastoring on Block Island, it became clear to me that the culture of the congregation regarding stewardship was, in effect, a silent ceiling on our ministry's potential. I determined that pledging was an important part of future faithfulness for us. (Maybe a congregational culture that assumed tithing as a minimum would see pledging as a step backward, but for us it was a huge leap forward!) In many ways subtle or blatant the congregation had shielded itself from pledging and stewardship campaigns. Numerous special offerings, fundraisers, and inactive stewardship committees were culturally acceptable. Pledging was not.

I initiated a process (keying on "assessment" although I did not have that level of analytical tools at my disposal then) that started with the maintenance of the relevant existing cultural components. We kept on having special offerings and fundraising events. Then I convened a number of different stewardship committees, none of which were particularly effective, but which succeeded in educating their members to our dilemma. Then we started a Commitment Campaign. Families could return a Commitment Card for their giving for the upcoming year if they wished to. About twenty did. After a couple of years we pushed all families to sign and return the card—even if the amount was left blank—so we could all be a part of a supportive team. So we doubled our card returns, though a large fraction were blank. Newcomers saw that stewardship cards were a part of our congregation's culture! Gradually, it had become part of our way of doing things. Now thirteen years later, eighty- five families "pledge." Not all like it, but it is accepted as normal congregational behavior.

John Hostetler shares a story of a major change in an Amish community's culture in his book *The Amish*.[19] Most Amish communities do not use automobiles. Cars are viewed as "English" and evil. Some communities have accepted their use after a long internal struggle. But one community went from horses to cars virtually overnight. It seemed an impossible transformation. Hostetler dug into the social dynamics and found that for over a decade the members of that community had been in a process of "reframing" their beliefs about the destructiveness of automobiles. With little change in behavior (unlike the "assessment" story above), the Amish in that specific community had developed a whole new and tolerant attitude regarding car usage. So when their first member bought a car, instead of being censured, he became a role model. Virtually every family "went out and did likewise."

Any one (or more) of these approaches can be the mechanism of cultural change. Transforming congregational culture is slow, but substantial ministry, a ministry requiring a laborious process of acquiring skill, but well worth the price.

Resources for Further Study

Acheson, James., *The Lobster Gangs of Maine,* Hanover, NH: University Press of New England, 1988.

Cook, Walter L. *Send Us a Minister . . . Any Minister Will Do,* Rockland, ME: Courier of Maine, 1978. Avaiable c/o of Box D2, Black Island, RI 02807.

Cushman, James E., *Beyond Survival,* Parsons, WV: McCLain Printing Co., 1981.

Cushman, James E., *Evangelism in the Small Church,* Decatur, GA: CTS Press, 1988.

Dudley, Carl S. and Douglas Alan Walrath, *Developing Your Small Church's Potential,* Valley Forge: Judson Press, 1988.

Grierson, Denham, *Transforming a People of God,* Melbourne, Australia: The Joint Board of Christian Education of Australia and New Zealand, 1984.

Hopewell, James F., *Congregational Stories and Structures,* Philadelphia: Fortress, 1987.

Jurgensen, Barbara, *Oh Please . . . Not Bethlehem!* Lima, OH: Fairway Press, 1986.

Sample, Tex, *Blue-Collar Ministry Facing Economic and Social Realities of Working People,* Valley Forge, PA: Judson Press, 1984.

The Life Cycle of the Congregation

Forces at Work

Individual people are born, grow, mature, age, and die. This is no revelation, but it does bear the shorthand label, life cycle. As individuals spawn children they start on their own cycle of life, overlapping their parents. Thus until the Second Coming.

Psychologists such as Erik Erikson [20] have noted that certain specifiable attitudes, energies, tasks, and resolutions correlate with each successive stage of the individual's psychological growth, defining a psychosocial as well as a physical life cycle. For example, "generativity" is the successful attainment of a last stage of the life cycle, passing on one's own acquired wisdom in a constructive way and then passing on.

Erikson's schema is helpful for clarifying in broad strokes the individual's journey. It is functional for a pastor to have some clue as to where he or she is in his or her life cycle. For example, my life cycle "task" the first few years out of seminary was to acquire and demonstrate competence. I took on all the church tasks the congregation could identify and even created many of my own. Eighteen years later my life cycle task is more nurturing and equipping: declining jobs, handing over opportunities, helping others acquire and demonstrate *their* competence.

The life cycle concept can be developed in two additional directions. The concept of life cycle can be applied to the "life" of a project or relationship in which the individual is involved. Thus a soup kitchen has a life cycle. Our congregation ran a coffee house for a number of summers. It was born in great expectations, ate up a lot of resources, served its purpose, grew old, and died. One can choose to think of it as a program that failed, or as one that lived out its God-given life cycle.

The second direction in which we might productively apply the concept of life cycle is organizationally. Often, we think of organizations from local PTAs to the U.S. Congress as continuously existing, especially as there is no specified *life span* for the organization. But in fact organizations exhibit life cycle dynamics, too. One cynic says organizations go from a man with a mission to a movement to a machine to a monument!

Robert Dale has productively applied life cycle dynamics to local congregations in his book *To Dream Again*.[21] He pictures the life cycle as a bell curve: Birth then Growth (ascending), then Maturity (plateau), followed by Decline and Death (descending). The congregational life style runs parallel: Dreams, Beliefs, Goals, Structure (ascending), the Ministry (plateau), followed by Nostalgia, Questioning, Polarization, and Dropout (descending).

Let us walk through Dale's stages of congregational life cycle. Every congregation is founded through a *dream*, a vision of what God can do here and now. The people involved have certain strongly held, highly motivational core *beliefs*. These beliefs interacting with situational opportunities are embodied in *goals*. The energy of the dream flowing through the goals gives shape to an organizational *structure* that empowers ongoing *ministry*. But eventually the dream energy ebbs, people come on board for a variety of personal reasons, and the organizational focus blurs. Fewer resources flow into the group and its environment changes. Wistful longing for the good old days–*nostalgia*–sets in. Then *questioning* (what's wrong? who's to blame?) that leads to hostility, camps, and *polarization*. Finally, organizational *death* occurs.

Sources of Tension

The first source of tension occurs when the expectation of congregational continuity is held while the congregation is actually experiencing diminishment. The physical evidence of the individual's life cycle is denied by many. I've tried to pastor to eighty-year-olds who, by their own calculations, were never going to die. If such an obvious reality as physical death can be put out of mind, how easy is it for those who truly do love their church to expect "glacial continuity." But when the congregation has peaked and is slipping from nostalgia to questioning, when diminishment is being experienced, then stress results. Often poor pastoring is blamed. If this tack is taken by the congregation, then hostility, confrontation, and disruption are the forms stress takes. If this tack is taken by the pastor, then guilt, workaholic scheduling, or despair are the expressions of stress.

The second source of pastoral tension arises when the congregation is at one point in their life cycle while the pastor is at a very different one. When an elderly, nostalgic congregation hires a visionary first charge pastor, stress is guaranteed. And when a small, new start church hires a pre-retired, burned-out senior pastor to lead them to bigness while he has his eyes unalterably set on a rocking chair and a social security check, stress is also guaranteed.

The third source of pastoral tension—and the most potentially healthy, if the most difficult—occurs when the congregation wants to return to the structures and ministries that felt so good without going through re-visioning as the pastor keeps insisting. Here both pastor and congregation concur on the experience of diminishment and on the expectation of a returning. The crossing of energies occurs in the nature of the returning. The congregation wants to turn back, turn back the clock to the good old days. The pastor (and/or some new or visionary old members) want to turn again, turn anew to God's fresh call. Unfortunately, there are few short cuts to spiritual/congregational health; the longer road is almost always the faithful one.

Recourses for Transformation

To assist a congregation to dream again and find energy in a new vision, a two-fold process is recommended:

a.   What is our heritage? What have we done? Make a time line. What was going on around us? Who responded? How? What was their vision?

b.   What are our opportunities? What is going on around us now? What resources, skills, hopes are in the congregation today? What do we care about? What can we do about it?

Martin Saarinen, in his very helpful booklet *The Life Cycle of the Congregation,*[22] puts it this way:

> The primary intervention for a congregation in Decline is twofold. First, the congregation needs to reconstruct its corporate memory concerning those people, places, times and events which stand out as being significant, to recapture the dynamisms of agony and ecstasy, joy and sorrow, pleasure and pain which they contained, to see the holdover effect of those events, and to sense the story being lived out in its historical narrative. Second, the congregation needs to touch base again with its setting. What mandates for ministry are inherent in the demographic and other changes in the congregation and com- munity—whether anticipated or already occurring? Together, a re- awakened sense of those forces which had previously breathed life into the congregation and an adequate perception of the possibilities for ministry in the congregation and community may combine to produce the condition whereby the congregation can continue to participate in the representation of Christ in that place in some new way.

Robert Dale gives us an example of dreaming again from a church in a resort area that, though only six years old, was slipping into nostalgia! The pastor devised a seven-part, year-long plan to dream again. The seven strategies are as follows:

1. Recall and celebrate the congregation's history;
2. Preach on the doctrines of the church;
3. Establish a new member training program;
4. Share gifts through an arts festival;
5. Develop four new mission projects;
6. Envision a new dream through drama in worship;
7. Evaluate church program by fifty church leaders.

This is one example. Your strategies will differ, but a process involving memories, analysis, reorientation, brainstorming, and celebration is indicated. [23]

My congregation on Block Island went through a mini-experience of dreaming again a few years back. It happened like this. I had been concerned about a change in our posture toward mission in our community. We had made great strides in opening our hearts and hands, wallets and our church building for further ministry on our island. But we seemed to have hit high water and the tide was ebbing. Little things. The Trustees fussing over youth group behavior. A Sunday School teacher angry at parents who drop their kids off. The Ladies group complaining about AA not washing their coffee cups. (Further inquiry revealed AA's innocence and our church members' guilt!) Deacons not responding to a request for assistance. It seemed to come to a head on the issue of controlling the use of the building. The Trustees wanted to ask the Food Coop to distribute their food elsewhere because dragging cartons had scuffed up our floor. I prevailed on the Trustees to change the request to "investigate the availability of a viable site." The Food Coop took offense, and feathers were ruffled all around. Were we closing down, turning inward, backing away from mission? Had we burned ourselves out and lost our vision for a positive mission involvement in the community? Had we become more interested in preserving than in spending ourselves in Christ's call to help others? The signs seemed to say so.

Then came a covered dish supper one cold winter's night. It was a Heritage Night where we remembered some aspect of our past. The topic was "The Night the Church Burned Down." In 1944, our previous sanctuary burned and a number of members and townspeople shared their memories, photographs, artifacts, etc. In the course of the evening, someone asked about previous church buildings. Bit by bit the story came out that we had had four earlier buildings, that they had all burned at various times, and that none had been built on the same site. Why not? Wanderlust? Poor relations with neighbors? Zoning? Moving across the tracks? The absurdity of each possible reason caused the group to chuckle. Then it dawned on us that the successive locations of the church building followed the same sequence as the center of town: from protected inland location to a spot convenient to the fishing fleets on both shores, to the Old Harbor servicing both fishermen and tourists. Each rebuilding of the church put it again in the center of island life. Each rebuilding was a statement of concern for and ministry to our community. Each rebuilding was a statement of high and renewed commitment to mission in our town!

The dream to be a vital, leavening, serving presence in our community was dreamed again that night. Since that night, the number of AA meetings held in our church building has doubled. A program to help the elderly with minor home repairs was launched. The kindergarten moved to our Sunday school rooms while the public school was remodelled. But best of all, the spirit of ministry that had seemed to be slipping into old age was reborn in our congregation.

Resources for Further Study

Dale, Robert D., *To Dream Again,* Nashville, TN: Broadman Press, 1981.

Erikson, Erik H., *Childhood and Society,* New York: W.W. Norton & Co., 1950.

Saarinen, Martin F., *The Life Cycle of a Congregation,* Washington, DC: The Alban Institute, 1986.

Family Systems

Forces at Work and Sources of Tension

Family Systems Theory is an incredibly rich approach to understanding the dynamics of families and of a family of families (as congregations may be viewed). Because of this richness and breadth and its current popularity, we will do no more than touch the surface here. Yet even a modest exposure may prove beneficial to those not familiar with this approach.

The current form of family systems theory grew out of the realizations of counsellors and therapists that on many occasions treating their individual client was an exercise in futility for their dysfunction was less inherent to the individual undergoing the therapy and more a manifestation of the dysfunction of their whole family as a system. Rabbi Edwin Friedman successfully applied family systems theory to congregational dynamics in his seminal book *Generation to Generation*.[24] We will consider five topics from Friedman: the congregation as an emotional system, homeostasis, triangulation, nonanxious presence, and self-differentiation with connection.

The congregation is an emotional system. What does that mean? Let us first consider, briefly, the nature of a system. Science initially made much progress by attempting to look at things in isolation. A system approach takes the opposite tack. It looks at things in connectedness. It claims that the system functions qualitatively differently than its components. (i.e., the whole is greater than the sum of its parts.) And the components are interconnected so that a change in one part of a system necessarily incurs a change in other parts. Moreover, what is a component in one system is itself a system considered internally. For example, a cell is a system in its internal functioning, but a component in relation to its organ, etc. An emotional system is one composed of sentient parts, their relationships, and the resulting emotions. The energy of family systems is anxiety. Anxiety and its management is the force behind the observable patterns of family and congregational functioning.

Pastoral stress results from two common misapprehensions regarding the congregation as an emotional system. The first is to overlook its systemic nature; the second is to overlook its emotional nature. Pastors who think they can act unilaterally and unidirectionally are in for a lot of stress! Linear thinking says that an action has its cause and effect. Period. System thinking reminds us that each effect is a new cause, ad infinitum. Once in a previous incarnation as a naive pastoral idealist, I introduced a bylaw change moving the church's budget formulating process from the Trustees to the more representative Executive Board. The effect was to give more power to the congregation as a whole to shape our expenditures and so reflect evolving priorities. That effect in turn reduced the power of the Trustee chairman to control expenditures, which was the cause of a reactive effect: his undying opposition to everything I subsequently proposed! Because I failed to use systemic thinking, the intent to open up the process resulted simply in changing to whom it was closed. Second, much pastoral stress results when the pastor fails to realize that emotional systems exist to manage anxiety. Anxiety is the coin of common life. The naive expectation that we can live in an anxiety-free congregational system is itself a great anxiety generator! Can we come to peace with the fact that we can't be at peace!

Homeostasis refers to the systems desire to return to "normal" after any disturbance. Systems develop preferred ways of being and have an amazing capacity to stay in them as long as possible, and to return to them as soon as possible after any change. Descriptors such as culture, habit, inertia, scripts, we've-never-done-it-that-way-before, steady state, baseline, default, etc. seek to label in different ways the homeostatic phenomenon. Pastoral stress regularly results when the pastor ignores or misjudges the power of homeostatic forces. Persons, families, and congregations routinely say they want to be Christlike, but what they really want is to stay in their comfort zone. Homeostasis is our everyday god. This does not mean that change, discipleship, and/or transformation are not possible; for they are. It simply means that we do well to recognize ministry for the momentous task that it is.

Triangulation stems from limits in our ability to deal constructively with our anxiety and has the result of enmeshing individuals in less than healthy family dynamics. Anxiety doesn't evaporate like dew in the midday sun. It hangs around, motivating the individual to find a painless way to reduce his or her anxiety. Confronting the individual who occasions one's anxiety increases anxiety. Examining the nature of an anxiety-fraught relationship increases one's anxiety. But involving a third party in the anxiety both reduces the experience of anxiety and sticks them into the anxious goop. Like misery, anxiety loves company. If I can reduce my anxiety by giving it to you, it feels like a solution to me. Of course, because the source of the anxiety is not dealt with, I will experience ongoing anxiety and need to stick with my third party "solution."

Where triangulation exists (and where doesn't it?), it will always cross with an expectation of healthy, confronting, and forthright relationships. But pastors experience another level of stress. This occurs in the mistaken assumption that triangulation is ministry! To hear the intimate confessions and frustrations of one church member relative to another is seductive. Often professional triangulators are adept at presenting their anxiety transferral in the most innocent or even inviting packages. Sometimes pastors, needing to be needed, invite or even demand such entanglements. It might look like ministry, it might feel like ministry, but its fruit is unproductive. On occasion triangulation may serve the positive role of allowing an individual to express his or her anxiety in a safe environment before moving on to deal with it directly. That, though, is seldom the intention of triangulators. So true ministry attempts to replace triangulation with more mature, direct, and healthy means of anxiety response. Let us now consider two means of such transformation.

Recourses for Transformation

Nonanxious presence. Anxiety is not self-correcting. It is self-perpetuating. If transformation is to come into the dysfunctions of an emotional system, it will come when at least one party decides to play by different rules. Anxiety is an option. It is experienced so spontaneously and so fundamentally that we often forget that we can opt out of anxiety. Not easily, to be sure, nor quickly, nor in each and every occasion. But we can say NO to anxiety, especially the anxiety that others bring to us. We do not have to get hooked. And if hooked, we can disentangle ourselves. What a liberating day it was for me in my ministry when I came to see the anxieties of other people as their spiritual agenda to work on. I realized that I could not solve their problems, nor would I be ministering to them if I were to. I could stand by them, give specific help, offer affirmation and encouragement. And I could best do that if I didn't fall headlong into the problem with them! By being present but not anxious,

I could provide something solid for them to reach out to as they worked on their issues. Still, I often slide down the slippery bank of anxiety into their problem with them; sometimes I am able to maintain a precarious balance on the edge of the bank, only to hear them complain that I wasn't there when they needed me; sometimes my non-anxious presence is of help to them. But, when I can maintain the balance, it is of help to me! To say, "It's not my problem" in love, may be the best pastoral way to say, "I love you."

Being present but without anxiety is also transformational in the life of the congregation as a whole. In the story of the bylaw change I related earlier, I was highly invested in the outcome. It was my idea to broaden the involvement. I formulated the change. I was determined to make it happen. I brought much anxiety to the issue. Of course, I disguised all this in theological language, but I really gave the congregation only two options: vote for me or vote against me. Sometimes the issue is that loaded and battle lines have to be drawn, but very seldom, I suspect. The rest of the time we shape the situation with our anxiety. My anxiety left the Trustee chair to either fold or fight. I wonder, if I could have pres-ented the whole change without such blatant personal investment, whether a more constructive, more creative third alternative would have emerged. Well, I won the vote, but my anxiety was not reduced. I found myself fretting subsequently at a conference when I ran into an older pastor friend of mine. His innocent, How are ya? brought forth my bitter tale of bylaw bile. Yeah, he mused in a mellow way, we're going through some bylaw changes now, too. We weren't comfortable with our old bylaws, but we weren't sure what we should have in their place. So we decided to suspend our bylaws and convene working groups to figure out how we would like to be organized. I don't know exactly how it will shake down, but whatever it is, it will be what they figure they want.

How could he be so mellow, I wondered. This was the Kingdom of God we were shaping! But precisely because it was the Kingdom of God, he was nonanxious and trusting, while helping the process along with his presence and resourcing. Well, years have gone by and I now appreciate and, to an extent at least, approximate his posture. Whether this forward movement has come through faith or fatigue, we won't get into!

Self-differentiation with connection. Edwin Friedman writes

regarding the basic concept of leadership through self-differentiation: "If a leader will take primary responsibility for his or her own position as "head" and work to define his or her own goals and self, while staying in touch with the rest of the organism [congregation], there is a more than reasonable chance that the body will follow."[25] Thus the more the pastor is a growing and healthy person, the more likely the congregation will be moved toward greater health and maturity. Friedman explains that supporting mature stances (one's own included) rather than trying to correct immature ones has a greater likelihood of succeeding. And furthermore, "As long as the leader is trying to change his or her followers, the latter are in the 'catbird's seat.'"[26] However, if the congregational leader takes their own growth and walks out, the congregation cannot be moved. It is in the connection that growth for the congregation is possible.

Resources for Further Study

Friedman, Edwin H., *Generation to Generation: Family Process in Church and Synagogue*, New York: 7 The Guilford Press, 1985.

Steinke, Peter, *How Your Church Family Works: Understanding Congregations as Emotional Systems*, Washington, DC: The Alban Institute, 1993.

Conclusion

Congregational dynamics are exciting, interesting, fun, and challenging, especially when they are occurring in some other pastor's congregation! Stressful is often the word we would use as they happen in our own. This chapter aimed to equip a pastor to transform stress in the congregational arena into energy for positive pastoring. As Paul meant to say in Romans 5:20, "But where stress abounds, grace did much abound."

CHAPTER 6

Stress
and the Changing Environment

The final arena of stress concerns pastoral expectations and experiences in the community and culture surrounding the church. This is the Environmental Arena and foreign territory to many pastors and congregations. The naive expectation that the world surrounding one's congregation is the same as that surrounding one's last church or the church of one's youth or even the same church last year is shattered by daily experience. It is a brave new world out there, and we must do more than scratch our heads in confusion or withdraw into the congregation in a misguided quest for security. The world around our churches is in flux, but with understanding and a dollop of grace we might be able to transform stress into progress.

In this chapter we will attempt to analyze the whirling, swirling society around the church from five varying perspectives. Some will overlap, some point in a unique direction, but each will provide a handle on understanding the dynamics at work in the environment of your congregation. Hopefully, one or more will reveal how your expectations have crossed with your experience and allow you to turn stress into strength. For each of these perspectives I am indebted to friends who have labelled what they were experiencing. Carl Dudley considers the difference between affective and directional orientations to faith. For our generational analysis, we will follow Doug Walrath's cohort schema. Sherry Walrath joins Doug, then, in analyzing church posture relative to its community. Tex Sample delineates three operational cultures in American society and considers ways to cross these cultural lines. Finally, Loren Mead faces into the wind of economic and social diminishment and invites the church to become a truly mission church.

Faith Orientations

Forces at Work and Sources of Stress

You know the story. Old First Church was a bustling success into the
sixties. Then the members moved away, the neighborhood changed, and
Old First is on the verge of closing. Reasons—blame?—are offered:
shortsightedness, lack of compassion and mission zeal, traditionalism,
prejudice, ostrich-approach, and/or stubbornness. But there may be a
more insightful reason: orientation to faith.

Or again. The pentecostal church drew a sizable and faithful congregation from the farm and mill workers in their rural county. Thinking
they would grow larger as the suburbs sprawled in their direction, and
working toward that end with home visits and revivals, they were instead
confounded when the new residents started a Presbyterian church! Per-
versity? More likely, faith orientaion.

Carl Dudley[1] has distinguished two basic orientations to faith. The
first he calls Relational faith practiced by Affectional Christians (AC).
The second is Rigorous faith practiced by Directional Christians (DC).
The differences between these two orientations is evident in the chart he
presents:

Relational Faith

Faith is discovered within a believing community, symbolized in infant baptism. (Gospel-love precedes obligation.)

A community consciousness defines individuals, sustains the culture and provides a stabilizing framework that even the rebels must accept. (Group Spirit is larger than individuals who participate.)

In a world created good, group identity is engendered by remembering the struggles of the past and joys of the present. Group life provides a place to shed the exterior pressures of the world and to celebrate oneness in Spirit. (Celebration-release is the most prized feeling.)

Land, family, and geographic community form the physical foundation through which faith is shared and passed on. (Human conservation is central.)

Relational faith is sustained by a sense of continuity, tradition, rhythm, and flow of events that evoke a sense of permanence. (Continuity provides stability.)

God is "felt" to be in the midst of the community, identified with people, places, and particular ways of doing things. (God is immanent.)

Rigorous faith

Faith begins when the believer qualifies by acknowledging his or her need for God and promises to will one will with the Divine. (Obligation precedes gospel.)

The community is composed of individuals who agree to work together (contract) for individual rewards and for a common end. (The group is the sum of its participants.)

In a world of evil people, the believers must struggle to restrain sin and create a better future for all. Individual achievements are honored, especially those resulting from self-restraint and discipline. (Ascetic restraint is the most prized feeling.)

Personal mobility, individual effort, and tireless productivity provide evidence that faith is genuine. (Personal vocation is central.)

Rigorous faith prepares for change, welcomes a challenge, and finds satisfaction in measuring its gains. (Dynamic achievements provide the basis for confidence in the future.)

God is beyond time and space, touching each person individually and uniquely, by God's grace and believer's commitment. (God is transcendent.)[2]

It does not take too much imagination or reminiscing to sense the power of these orientations.   One's own orientation is right, and the other's not exactly Christian! Again Dudley compares perceptions:

Affectional Christian with Relational Faith

Column I	Column II
Affirms him/herself with the following self-perceptions:	Misunderstands the Directional Christian with the following misperceptions:
1. We belong naturally to a church home and a congregational church.	They are independent, lonely, and difficult to know. "He keeps his distance."
2. We easily contribute our thoughts and feelings to the group as an extension of ourselves, sustained by God.	They are ambitious, which makes them appear impatient, competitive, and domineering. "You are always so busy."
3. We live on people-time, emphasizing who is present rather than program activity.	They appear to be judging the group by reducing the people to numbers and programs to productivity. "Our people have names, not numbers."
4. We grow as a group by increased intimacy of members and sensitivity to the whole.	They try to arouse us to make changes that do not seem possible or advisable. "We tried that last year."
5. We know the immanence of God in the traditions of worship.	They have not experienced God as we have, and always keep experimenting. "We wish you were here longer."

Directional Christian with Rigorous Faith

Column III	Column IV
Misunderstands the Affectional Christian with the following misperceptions:	Affirms him/herself with the following self-perceptions:
1. They appear aimless, disorganized, and disinterested in changing the world. "They are irresponsible."	We join by responding to the challenge to do our share in the building of God's Kingdom.
2. They appear hung up on past events and personal experiences. "They appear clannish and out of date."	We know we belong in the ordered universe by organizing our lives and our share of the Kingdom.
3. They appear too emotional and immature as a group. "They are no different from the world, simply a social club, not Christians."	We plan and work with the faith that God blesses believers with success.
4. They are survival-oriented, passive, and used by others. "They have no prophetic ministry."	We believe that God is at work changing people and affecting history.
5. They have not been told the Truth, or have not heard it spoken with power. "They need enlightenment."	We believe in a God who transcends history, and who loves and judges each of us equally, separately.[3]

Stress occurs, then, when a church of primarily one orientation attempts to relate to a surrounding population of primarily the other orientation. Finding people of such a faith can be as stressful as encountering neighbors of no faith!

Recourses for Transformation

Recourses for positively responding to differences in faith orientation
fall into two categories: *vive la difference* and *integrative.*

Vive la difference

Acknowledging the fundamental difference between these two orientations to faith, a congregation may come to peace with its own identity
while at the same time serving as a feeder for a congregation of the other
orientation. For example, any DCs that find themselves in an AC congregation could be invited to attend the sister congregation (DC). That
congregation might return the favor. Because congregations and pastors
tend to want to be all things to all people and view each other somewhat
competitively, I doubt this recourse will be much tried. But it has some
theoretical niceties. A more likely variant is to develop two congregations within one church structure. The ACs can meet in the soundproof
chapel on Sunday night while the DCs do all things decently and in
order at 11 a.m. in the sanctuary.

Integrative

This recourse involves deliberate and difficult effort to integrate the two
orientations. Much education, dialogue, compromise, and patience will
be required. The successful congregation, though small, will undoubtedly become very spiritually mature.

Attempts at evangelism are significantly influenced by the AC/DC
match/mismatch. Historic efforts by DCs to convert ACs to Christ typically result in minimal numbers converted to DC orientation, rather
than Christ, as witness white missionaries to the Native Americans. And
one is hard put to cite any historic evidence of ACs' success in convert-
ing DCs. Evangelistic efforts are most successful within orientations.
When trying to communicate across AC/DC lines, affirmation of the
other orientation and providing a place to live it out seem to be minimal
ingredients if there is to be any success.

Resources for Further Study

Dudley, Carl S., *Affectional and Directional Orientations to Faith*, Washington, DC: The Alban Institute, 1982.

Cohorts—Generational Differences

Forces at Work

One way that the environment around the church is changing has to do with generational sequence. Once we could assume continuity from one generation to another. Kids do what adults did at their age. This is clearly not true in American society today. There is indeed a generation gap. Doug Walrath[4] calls these age-differentiated groups "cohorts." He delineates three major cohorts in American society today: Strivers, Challengers, and Calculators. These approximate the three adult generations the church can relate to.

Strivers are the oldest of the adult generations, most in their pre-retirement and retirement years. Strivers believe in the American Dream, the good life, and that it can be achieved by personal effort and work—striving. Strivers' attitudes were shaped by the two world wars and the intervening depression. A deacon aptly describes a striver in our congregation in saying, "His wife won't let him go to the dump. He always brings back more than he takes!" Even though he has built five outbuildings to house all this stuff, his depression-formed waste not-want not mentality drives him still. Duty, respectability, and loyalty are quintessential Striver values.

Challengers are virtually identical to the Baby Boomers, born after World War II. Formative events/realities in their lifetime include increased mobility and affluence, suburbia, the Civil Rights movement, hula hoops and the Beatles, urban crises, assassinations, and the Vietnam war. The sanguine preconscious moral framework of Strivers has been challenged by this succeeding generation. Flag burning, bra burning, free sex, alternative lifestyles, and bold music are all expressions of their challenging of the status quo. Immediacy, internal validation, and personal experiences are quintessential Challenger values.

Calculators have been shaped by events from roughly 1970 on: Kent State shootings, gasoline shortages, widespread divorce, ERA, Three Mile Island, shuttle and Chernobyl explosions, terrorism, and hostages. Calculators believe the pie to be shrinking and are calculating about grabbing at least their fair share. The optimism of the Strivers regarding the future is completely gone among Calculators. Limitations, competition, erosion, and constraints are quintessential Calculator realities.

How Cohorts Approach Living

Strivers	*Challengers*	*Calculators*
Stability is normal	Change is normal	Erosion is normal
Defend our way of life	Alter and expand our way of life	Choose and conserve what matters most
Alternatives	Options	Consequences
Oughts; begin with obligations	Wants; begin with interests	Possibilities; begin with constraints [5]

At a recent Executive Board meeting of my congregation, the pain of cohort clash was in evidence. We met to review the special events of the summer and make some plans for next summer. Instead we spent a lot of time listening to the complaint of the chair of the Fair against the chair of the Walk for Hunger. "First she would jump up immediately after I made my announcement [during Sharing Time in worship]. Sunday after Sunday, it got frustrating. Then when I asked her about it she said, 'Well, people remember what they hear last.' Doesn't that beat all?"

Strivers would work hard on both the fair and the walk, believe in an expanding pie, and trust all would win. Challengers would work on fair or walk, which ever was meaningful to them and be perfectly pleased to let others get involved however they wished. But only a Calculator would plan to speak after another, hoping to push out the other message. Competing against other church members and activities for limited dollars is a Calculator perspective. By meeting's end we had decided to do both the fair and the hunger walk again next year and to have the same person chair each again. Somehow between now and then I am going to have to learn some inter-cohort confliction resolution skills!

Sources of Stress

These three cohorts comprise three radically different worlds–language, customs, values, motivations so different as to reduce cross-cohort dialogue to near zero levels. The typical mainline Protestant American congregation is still composed of a majority of grey-haired Strivers complaining about the lack of religious practice of their Challenger children, and completely befuddled by the appeal of charismatic-type churches to their grandchildren. Their Challenger children reject Striver religion as loyalty-based, externally formulated, and intrapersonally repressive, whereas Calculator grandchildren find joyful, cathartic, and emotional religious expressions well worth the hour or two a week. The expectation of successive generational involvement in "church" and the experience of low attendance stresses many congregations.

A second source of stress occurs when the pastor is of one cohort and the congregation primarily of another. Typically, the pastor is a Challenger challenging Strivers in ways they don't appreciate!

A third source of stress occurs when a Striver congregation finds themselves in an environment of Challengers and Calculators. Must such a congregation adopt a Masada-esque defense against the encroaching apostasy and await either decimation or self-destruction? Are there no ways to establish dialogue and offer the salvation of Christ in terms comprehensible to other cohorts?

Recourses for Transformation

In his book *Options*,[6] Doug Walrath shows in detail how churches can, with effort and courage, talk and minister across cohort lines. We will present some broad stroke suggestions.

1. **Develop a tolerant attitude toward other cohorts.** The presumption of self-righteousness is always illusory, none the less so generationally. Strivers' spirituality undoubtedly ranks higher to Strivers than

to the Divine. If each cohort can adopt a modest attitude toward their spiritual practices and a tolerant, inquiring or open-minded one toward the others', communication would be furthered.

2.   **Believe that the Holy Spirit has been at work before us !** Imagine God doing things without running it through us! Rather impertinent of El Divino, wouldn't you say? We church-y types remind me of the disciples hurrying to get Jesus to silence one who was healing in Jesus' name, but not in their camp. Jesus educates them: "He who is not against us is for us!" (Mark 9:40) God is at work in all cohorts. More discerning and less criticizing might help.

3.   **Become familiar with Cohort Perspectives.** A foreign missionary learns at least a little of the country's language and world view. We can do no less if we expect to share good news with other cohorts. This chart summarizes some of the key thought, language, and behavior differences across cohorts.

How Cohorts Approach Believing and the Church

Strivers	*Challengers*	*Calculators*
God is taken for granted	God is defined personally and is optional	God is defined and seen as essential by believers only
Church is central, a stabilizing force	Church is marginal, a social advocate	Churches play a variety of roles
Morality predominates	Ethics predominate	Piety predominates
Expect to support church and be cared for; to be loyal to church; to belong	Expect church to support my needs and causes; to find meaning from church; to act	Expect church and be church to nurture and support; to gain resources from church; to survive[7]

4. **Enter Their World.** Create points of contact. If they won't cross the church's threshold, go out and engage them where they are. A covered-dish supper hosted by a church bridged the gap between Strivers and Challengers in one rural town.[8] Forms and strategies will vary. What is virtually universal is that other cohorts won't come onto your turf on their own energy; you must go onto theirs, or at the very least, find ways to open up to them.

5. **Structure for Other Cohorts.** Once contact is made, honor the other cohorts by structuring around their approach. We have created an alternative worship format in our congregation—with modest success—to coordinate with the posture of Challengers and to some degree Calculators. It has these features:

a. Contemporary **language** replaces traditional language as much as possible, e.g., spiritual, not religious, maturity more than sanctification.

b. Experiences are designed to be **personal** not impersonal, e.g., small group sharing.

c. The desired style is **active** not passive. Each person is viewed as a contributor to the experience, not a passive recipient of another's wisdom. Interactive exercises are better than unilateral. Dialogical communication is preferred to monological. Involving the whole person, not just the left brain, is the goal.

d. **God** is understood as immanent primarily and transcendent secondarily. The locus of the Kingdom is seen as within. Guided meditation is a means of helping to discover God already at work within our souls.

e. God's **truth** is to be apprehended by the whole brain, not the left brain only. Bible passages are acted out, not simply read. Attempts are made to integrate ideas, feelings, and actions.

f. **"Sin"** is seen as other- and self-destructive scripting more than individual transgression. Nonconformity to given structures is seen as less evil than the nonfulfillment of one's God-given spiritual potential.

g.   The **structure** is do-able for Challengers and Calculators. The meeting is midweek, short, with meal and child care provided.

Even so, not all persons of other cohorts will hear the message, but at least we will be talking in a similar language.

Resources for Further Study

Owens, Owen D., *Growing Churches for a New Age,* Valley Forge, PA: Judson Press, 1981.

Walrath, Douglas Alan, *Frameworks: Patterns of Living and Believing Today,* New York: The Pilgrim Press, 1987.

Walrath, Douglas Alan, *Options: How to Develop and Share Christian Faith Today,* New York: The Pilgrim Press, 1988.

Church Type

Forces at Work

Doug and Sherry Walrath offer us a simple yet helpful method of categorizing churches into three types depending on how they are perceived by those in their environment. They label these three types Dominant Church, Denominational Church, and Distinctive Church. This schema is useful in that it asks the concerned church leader to place him- or herself outside of the church and assess it from that perspective. It also explains a large amount of pastoral stress, opening avenues for constructive response.

Walraths' Dominant Church is the tall-steepled, prestigious church attended by those who count, or want to, in a given community. Its middle (or higher) class members desire competent leadership, quality programs, and a well-maintained, functional building. The well-being of this church, though, is tied to the economic and social changes affecting the community at large. It waxes and wanes accordingly. It is perceived by many in the community as sufficient unto itself, a "bastion," and not a welcoming place. This image keeps new people away, sometimes the very people the congregation would like to reach.

The second type, the Denominational Church, is based on its members loyalty and identification with one denomination. This type of church is susceptible to demographic change and the generation gap in denominational loyalty. The Denominational Church is also tied to economic and social trends, but not as closely as the Dominant Church. This church is perceived to be for Methodists or Southern Baptists only, and so the denominational image is a barrier to relating to and attracting people of other backgrounds in its environment.

The Distinctive Church is the third type. This church is known for a specific emphasis. Some examples are charismatic, fundamentalist, and social action, but the emphases may vary widely. This type of church is more likely to draw like-minded people from a much wider area than the other two types of churches. It tends to function outside of the influence of economic or social trends. Interestingly, if it is influenced by societal movements, the correlation is often a negative one. Thus if the regional economy suffers, this type of church may well gain in membership and income!

Sources of Stress

Pastoral stress occurs when the pastor's expectations are mismatched with the perceptions of the people in the church's environment and, for that matter, within the congregation itself. Thus if a pastor feels that his or her authority and identity are lodged in the apostolic succession of the Anglican church, but the people in a rural county see that Episcopal church as the only place of worship for miles and thus a house of prayer for all peoples, tension and stress are in the making. In my early years of pastoring on Block Island, I attended a conference that was supposed to teach me how to make my church successful. The leader had made his suburban church successful by specializing his ministry and being very intentional about doing only those things that would directly lead to success. "For example," he said, "I get plenty of requests for weddings to which I always say no unless the couple are church members. Let them get married in a church that doesn't know where it's going—there are plenty of those around." Hmmm, I thought, if I told a Block Island

couple to go find another church, that I didn't have time for them, I
would soon have plenty of time. For neither they nor their relatives, nor
their friends would come to church unto the third and fourth generations.
Three or four non-weddings and I'd be a man of leisure, having a clear
idea of where I was going—into unemployment! His church type was
distinctive, and his strategy appropriate for that type. My church falls
into the dominant category, not because we're prestigious but because
for us everyone counts. We are a community church, and to act otherwise would be to create enormous quantities of stress.

Recources for Transformation

Dominant, Denominational, and Distinctive are easily identifiable categories for pastors and church leaders to utilize. These categories consti-
tute one of the most user-friendly self-**analysis** tools available. Coming
to an awareness of how one's congregation is perceived by its community will also reveal the entry points and barriers to entry felt by others in
the community. This can be better done by adding community question-
naire or interview results to the impressions of members. We do not
always see ourselves as others see us!

Second, it is important to come to peace with the congregation's
identity. Each of these types represents a faithful posture. Yet God also
calls churches to change their type. A denominational church in a region
of economic diminishment and church closings may find itself called to
expand its identity and become more of a community-dominant type
chuch. Or a dominant church of a village which finds itself now a
hinterland for a Wal-Mart town[9] may chose to follow God's leading into
a distinctive posture. Whatever type each congregation is or is becoming, it must come to **acceptance** of this identity or its conflictedness will
preclude effectiveness.

Third, take **action.** If a congregation is the local Presbyterian fran-
chise, be that! If a congregation sees itself as existing for the community,
then be that. Open your doors to community groups; do all those weddings turned down by the suburban-success-distinctive types. Align your
energy with your identity and stress will be replaced by exhiliration!

Resources for Further Study

Walrath, Doug and Sherry, "Supporting Small Congregations and Their Pastors," *The Five Stones,* Vol. 12, No. 1 (Winter 1994): 2-4. Reprinted from *The Open Door,* Bangor (ME) Theological Seminary.

Cultures: Left, Middle, and Right

Forces at Work

At an executive board meeting of my congregation a couple of years ago, a very interesting question was posed. What is our faith for? What does Christianity do for us? I jumped to the bait and launched into an exhaustive and utterly compelling (or so I thought) description of faith as the energy to go forward in the Lord's will, to grow in grace, to learn from every experience, to chart our course by Christ's counsel, and to never be the same person tomorrow that I was yesterday. It was a pure and sincere expression of my operational theology. It also was a pure and sincere expression of journey theology and marked me as a card carrying member of the cultural left. I didn't expect the Second Coming to occur on the spot, but neither did I expect the great big clunk from our board members that followed. Finally, Jack T. spoke up. "Well, I guess I don't quite see it that way. Christianity helps me make the right decisions. When we're faced with different ways to go, one is right or at least more right, and my Christian faith helps me to make that choice." Gertrude F. then spoke. "My Christian faith gives me the strength to get through the day. I have a difficult job, troubles with customers, troubles with employees. If I couldn't pray to Jesus at any moment, I'd never make it to quitting time."

We went on with the meeting's agenda, but those two comments, especially after what I had thought to have been the definitive theological word, gave me much cause for reflection. It was only later after reading Tex Sample's *U.S. Lifestyles and Mainline Churches* [10] that I had the cognitive tools to help me interpret what had happened at that meeting. Sample says that there are three cultures that operate within American society today. He labels these left, middle, and right. Those in the cultural left are predominantly baby boomers. They come from affluent families and are characterized by a sense of inner direction and a drive for self-fulfillment. They desire personal freedom for themselves and accord a laissez faire pluralism to others.

Those in the cultural middle come primarily from the traditional middle class. In this group career and achievement are highly emphasized. They attempt to live out the ideals lifted up by the American culture of the past. People in the cultural middle exhibit a utilitarian individualism that leaves many feeling isolated and lonely. They are highly self-conscious and intensely personal. They take an active stance towards life and are much more likely to attempt to do God's will than to be still and accept God's grace. Cultural middle people tend to practice "invisible religion" and participate in congregations of civility, that is, churches in which politeness and privacy are practiced as the primary virtues.

The cultural right is comprised of the poor and the working lower middle class. These people tend to approach life on an immediate, short term basis. They are territorially rooted and are oriented towards local, grassroot realities. They emphasize traditional values: family, flag, and conventional morals.

Sample's categories helped me to see that Jack T. was articulating the theological perspective of the cultural middle, and Gertrude F. the cultural right. No matter how eloquent I might have waxed about my cultural left theology, I was on a different wave length.

Sources of Stress

Expecting parishioners to be of the same culture is one source of pastoral stress. Expecting one's congregation to be purely of one culture may lead to a second source of pastoral stress. However, the stress I would like to focus on concerns the expectation that the pastor and congregation are of the same culture as their social environment. Undoubtedly, most Protestant congregations are in the cultural middle. Cultural middle folk tend to see people of the cultural right as lazy, unorganized, and unresponsive to spirituality. They tend to see people of the cultural left as selfish and without a sense of duty and loyalty. These perspectives lead them to desire to convert those around them to their own cultural position rather than attempting to minister to them as legitimately different. And it is confusing for religious folk of the cultural middle when other members of their culture are not interested in invisible religion or joining congregations of civility.

Recourses for Transformation

What would ministry look like if your congregation were to attempt to incarnate Christ's grace in terms each culture could understand? Ministry to those of the cultural left would attempt to address specific life issues. It would not emphasize pie in the sky or abstract theological concepts, but truths of immediate relevancy and practical usefulness. Life would be articulated as a journey, and faith would be seen as revealing the spiritual dimensions of that journey. Personal integrity and God's presence in all things would be emphasized.

Ministry to the cultural middle would start by focusing on the personal pain experienced by this group and respond in the form of healing and support groups. The theological enterprise would be explanatory, helping people to understand their everyday activities in light of God's purpose for them. Tools and resources to help move private faith into one's public contexts would be provided.

Ministry to the cultural right would require a shift in cognitive perspective. Truths would not be expressed as abstract principles of justice but incarnated in conventional lifestyles. Theology would not take the form of explanation or a journey, but that of folk theology. Religion is seen as a way of life more than a view of life. God is immediately involved in the events of one's life and yet is most often approached through mediators. The world is seen as a hostile place and faith impacts directly on basic personal needs. In practice, prayer is a mechanism for obtaining specific favors from God. Religion is oral, not literate.[10]

Responding constructively to the reality of these three cultures is not an easy thing for a congregation. The simplest option is to specialize in one culture only, live it out fully, and consign the other two to the judgment of God or, more positively, another congregation. However, some congregations will find themselves multicultured internally or feel called to minister in a culturally pluralistic environment. These churches will try to offer something that appeals to each culture and implement this strategy in their staffing and programming. These congregations will need clergy and lay leaders who are bi- or trilingual and can function in each culture. The method that can produce such quality leadership awaits development.

Shannon Jung [11] offers a practical first step for leaders of a local church. "They might construct a chart with three columns. They could summarize the characteristics of the congregation in the first, the values of the congregation's different lifestyle groups in the second, and the ways in which the church is responding to those values and concerns in the third column. That might suggest future directions or emphases. A second sort of analysis could do the same thing for the residents of the town or larger community in which the church is located."

Owen Owens shares a more personal approach. He had heard of a church in rural Massachusetts in which the long-time members (cultural right) had developed a significant rapport and a number of cooperative efforts with some radical twenty-somethings (cultural left). So he went to investigate. What he found was a congregation that was open to some new ideas and even some new people from time to time. (In fact, this social openness harked back nearly two hundred years and the congregation kept alive and well their memory of this heritage.) And he found a pastor who built bridges, feeling that God may have a blessing for the congregation in these folk with different lifestyles. As he visited with the cultural left people, he found that they did not all know each other and desired a forum to discuss their alternative values. So the pastor offered them a place to meet monthly: the church. They responded and vital sharing began. Soon others started attending. After a while the monthly meetings evolved into a community supper in which people from both cultures broke bread together, got to know each other in deeper ways, and developed enough trust and mutual respect to work together on community projects! [12]

Resources for Further Study

Jung, L. Shannon, "Review of U.S. Lifestyles and Mainline Churches," *The Five Stones,* vol. 9, no. 1 (Winter 1991): 17-19.

Ong, Walter J., *Orality and Literacy,* New York: Routledge, 1982.

Owens, Owen D. *Growing Churches for a New Age*, Valley Forge, PA: Judson Press, 1981.

Sample, Tex, *U.S. Lifestyles and Mainline Churches*, Louisville, KY: Westminster/John Knox Press, 1990.

Cultural	Left
Who	Baby Boomers
Characteristics	Inner directed Self-fulfillment From affluent families Committed to personal freedom for self Pluralism for others
Church Strategies	Focus on specific life issues Immediate relevancy Faith as journey Emphasize integrity, God in all

Middle	Right
Traditional Middle Class	Poor, Working People (lower middle class)
Emphasize career and achievement Live out ideals of culture Utilitarian individualism leaves feelings of loneliness and isolation Highly self-conscious Intensely private Active stance toward life Do God's will Accept God's grace Reflect commercial base of bourgeois existence Congregation of civility Invisible religion	Short-term approach Local, territorially rooted orientation Emphasize traditional values— family, flag, conventional morals Local folkways
Focus on Pain— healing/support groups Explanatory Theology— understanding everyday activities re: God's will Move private faith into public context	Conventional lifestyles not justice principles Folk theology

Societal Shifts

Forces at Work

Today's church is like the couple that went on a trip. While they were
gone a moving van pulled up, took all their old furniture, and put in new
furniture in new places. When the couple came home carrying their
same old baggage, not paying any attention, they tripped over the new
furniture placement. Sprawled on their backs, they looked around not
only to see new furniture in new places, but also to realize that they were
not "at home" anymore.

The church isn't in the place it used to be. American culture isn't
where it used to be either. There has been a major shift in society.
People are more mobile and affluent. They live in different places and
believe different things. The whole architecture of community life has
changed. As recently as a half century ago, life was structured differently from today. Then the local town or village was central. Now
people drive to work and worship. They shop and play anywhere in a
very large region. Then life had a feeling of wholeness with a stable cast
of characters and a known script. Today life is lived in bytes and bits
with different people doing new things. Then life was simple. Now it is
complex. Then the pace was slow. Now it is fast. Then the church was
prominent and accessible. Now the church is but one remote option.[14]

Where does this leave the local church? Once the church could be
assumed to have power or at least a place of significance in the society of
its community. Today there are far more people at shopping malls than
at church on a Sunday morning. Certainly churches continue to exist, but
they have slid to the periphery of society. Churches are perceived by
some as benign but insignificant, by others as throwbacks to an unliber-
ated age, by others as relics of an irrelevant past, by others as antithetical
to progress, by others as an opiate, and only by a small minority as a vital
center for healing, justice, and meaning. Churches once central are now
peripheral.

And pastors, where are we? Most likely the pastor you grew up with
was placed on a pedestal, even by non-Christian elements in the community. He was accorded place and respect and discounts on railroads and
ferry boats. He spent a lot of time giving character references to the
bankers and prayers to the Lions or Rotarians. Once he was on a pedestal,

but now we have been relegated to the Pumpkin Patch, with other
Charlie Browns, waiting for the never appearing Great Pumpkin! Try
to speak words of significance from a pumpkin patch.

The great shifts in American society have moved the church from the
center of society to the periphery, from the mainstream to the margin.

Sources of Stress

So? In other places and other times the church of Jesus Christ has lived
at the margin of society and did not suffer undue stress about it. In fact,
many times it thrived at the edge. But that church had different expectations. We expect a place of high status and are embarrassed and stressed
to be ushered to a back seat at this wedding feast. We aspired to that
position of power and significance, the pastorate of our youth, but when
we grab at it, it disintegrates in our grasp. We remember when one
couldn't graduate without a Baccalaureate, but now pastors aren't even
invited to graduation. We expected to be Somebody in the eyes of society, but we have been "reduced" to the quest to be Somebody in the eyes
of God. This is the spiritual stress related to the shifts in society. But
there is also sociological stress.

We expected a role in the center of things, with access to the Oval
Office. We expected to be chaplains to the mighty military-industrial
complex. We expected a society that reinforced our values and world
view, that delivered people to our services, committees, and potluck
suppers. Instead we have been left in the breakdown lane. Society has
zipped past us and doesn't seem to hear us over the roar, no matter how
loud we yell. We don't have a platform for our platitudes anymore. We
experience our place at the margin as crossing with our expectations of
the pastoral role as central, powerful, and respected. We don't even have
the expectation that there are roles of power and faithfulness and effec-
tivess and transformation at the margin, and so it is stress that we feel
instead of exhilaration and satisfaction.

And there is psychological stress when we live at the margin. We
know how to do church at the center. We know what that church feels
like and how we feel when the church and the society are aligned. We
know how to do that kind of church. But how do you do church at the
margin? We don't know. To get four years of college and three of

seminary under our belts and out of our bank accounts only to realize we
are now prepared for jobs and pastoral roles that no longer exist, now
that is stress, stress and anger, or more often denial. It is less stressful to
do what we know how to do even though deep down we know that it will
no longer do. It is less stressful, at least at the beginning, but it is also
less faithful, less functional, and less fulfilling.

Recourses for Transformation

What to do? Well, first why don't we accept reality? The church of the
twenty-first century is the church at the margin of society. Wishing it
weren't so won't change us back. It will only debilitate us.

Second, if we are at the margin, might not God have had a hand in
that? Why don't we accept our place at the margin as God's will? Why
don't we embrace the new possibilities, the new adventure, the challenge
of digging new wells, not dusting off those old dry wells of our forefa-
thers? (Genesis 26:18) God is establishing our congregations as mission
outposts at the margins of society. Imagine, we no longer have to send
missionaries. We are missionaries! We are now God's guerillas, armed
with a subversive vision of a cause so powerful it is out of this world.
We can have the same fun the twelve apostles did, the same excitement
recorded in the book of Acts, the same quest that propelled Paul, the
same opportunity as Peter to create a people to God. (I Peter 2:10) Of
course, one has to see our new place at the margin as gain and not loss,
and expect God's blessing, not curse, and experience small strides
toward the Kingdom as momentous accomplishments.

Third, we need to find new ways of envisioning, functioning, and
traning for marginal, missionary endeavors. That book hasn't been
written yet. The Holy Spirit is writing it in pieces,[16] a chapter in hearts
here and there. Maybe in your heart!

Stress comes to pastors when they expect the social environment
around the church to reinforce their expectation of a social religion. You
were born a few decades too late! But exhilaration comes when one accepts the church's place at the margin as a mission outpost and gets on
with the mission.

Resources for Further Work

Mead, Loren B., *The Once and Future Church, Reinventing the Congregation for a new Mission Frontier*, Washington, DC: The Alban Institute, 1991.

Mead, Loren B., *Transforming Congregations for the Future*, Bethesda, MD: The Alban Institute, 1994.

Pappas, Anthony G. and Scott Planting, *Mission: The Small Church Reaches Out,* Valley Forge, PA: Judson Press, 1993.

Strobel, David and Darrell Jodock, "Ministry in an Unmapped Society, *Lutheran Partners* (May/June 1994).

CHAPTER 7

Beyond Stress?

You've come to the end of a book on stress. You will go beyond this book, but there is no going beyond stress. There is no outgrowing stress, no reaching stress free-ness. The only stress-free people are those in the cemetery. (At least, we hope and pray they are!) But in this realm stress is for sure and forever. So what are we going to do with it?

The story is told of an Oriental potentate who desired to test the maturity of his three sons. For some inscrutable reason he decided to do this by placing a raw egg on the top of the slightly ajar door to his throne room and then inviting each in turn to enter. The youngest son, eager but naive and insensitive, walked right through the door and caught the egg full on his face! The middle son, more aggressive and wary, opened the door, sensed something falling, drew his sword and smashed egg all over the room! After the mess was cleaned up, the eldest son was called. He opened the door, sensed the dropping egg and caught it gingerly. He thanked his father for providing supper and went on his way.

We have stepped through the door of pastoring, and the egg is falling. The question is, what are we going to do with it? We can proceed in ignorance and naivete about the forces of stress in our pastorate, but we are likely to end up with egg on our face. We can slash at stress, rail and fight against it, but all we are likely to achieve is a large mess. Or we can embrace the stress we encounter in pastoring, embrace it and let it nourish our pastoring.

How can one embrace stress? How can one be nourished by stress?

Stress is an invitation to coordinate with God's agenda. If you are a goal-oriented person, interruptions are more than interruptions in schedule, agenda, or energy; they are irritations, frustrations, and time and energy wasters. In the face of our definition of self, ministry, and agenda, God is offering us the divine agenda and it comes to us in the guise of stress. Stress is present to teach us that the interruptions in our agenda *are* our spiritual ministry agenda. We (I am chief) often resist this invitation to redefine our ministry focus until the pain of stress forces us into redefinition.

So stress is a divine red tag that reads: Minister here! The ministry may be in the person (soul) of the pastor, in the culture of the congregation, or with elements in the environment, or some combination. But stress can be embraced as a ministry focus indicator. Stress speaks God's agenda if we would but listen.

Similarly, stress tells us not only what God would have us *do*, but also who God would have us *be*. God would have us be in touch, in communication, in love with the divine Spirit. Stress is the invitation to live in God's grace. Stress invites us to invite God in. If we resist long enough, stress will drive us to our knees begging God's redemptive, rescuing presence. But why wait? Why not use stress' first pangs to go immediately into God's presence to ask right away the meaning of the message our eternal Partner is sending us in stress' early emergence? Prayer, meditation, personal Bible study, fellowship with honest spirits in warm, interpersonal places are some of the forms in which our God connection may grow at the goad of increasing stress. Stress itself may not nourish our spirit, but it invites us to receive the nourishment of God's presence.

So stress befriends us, and we can befriend stress and embrace its potential for personal growth. Stress' energy can be an impetus for our spiritual growth and personal maturity. Stress is energized by some incompleteness in our understanding and attitude. Stress is our own inner cry to fill and fulfill ourselves. Stress is our soul's plea to move on toward the "maturity of Jesus Christ." (Eph. 4:13) Stress will be our friend if we embrace it as a blessing in disguise.

Of all the realities that are labelled stress, we have explored one. We have examined stress as crossed energy, the emotional energy that is the result of a pastor's expectations crossing with his or her experience. We have considered crossed energy in five pastoral arenas: personal, interpersonal, role-related, congregational, and environmental. Our claim is that when crossed energy can be aligned, when one's understanding and expectations become consonant with the realities out there, then stress is transformed into strength, breakdowns into breakthroughs, and energy is released for growth and ministry.

I have attempted to make this book as broad as possible, but even so it is nowhere near covering the whole waterfront. It is my hope that, through these specifics, an attitude toward stress and an approach to life that will lead us to utilize the stress in our lives to advance our growth and ministry has been demonstrated. I hope this book has primed your pump regarding a positive response to stress and that you can go from here and grow far beyond these elementary thoughts.

Hidden in each stress is a spiritual treasure. If you will swallow only sweet experiences of growth, the Holy Spirit's work in your life will be greatly restricted. But to paraphrase scripture, the stress that is bitter to taste can be very sweet to digest, and from such stress can come great spiritual nourishment and pastoral ministry.

May God bless you as you experience the spiritual treasure hiding in each stress.

NOTES

Chapter 2

1. Walter Ong suggests that the shift from orality to literacy has reduced the capacity to "hear" internal voices. See Ong, *Orality and Literacy* (New York: Routledge, 1982). I am not suggesting that we listen for voices, but for messages, truths, thoughts, feelings, and reactions within our souls. In these messages, God's truth may be discernible.

2. Carl Jung, ed., *Man and His Symbols* (New York: Dell Publishing Co., 1964), 92

3. Frank Waters, *Book of the Hopi* (New York: Penguin Books, 1963), 9-10. Used by permission of Viking Penguin, a division of Penguin Books USA, Inc.

4. Robbie Klein Lonewold, "The Best of Many Worlds", *Douglass Alumnae Bulletin* (Spring, 1990), 9.

5. Owen Owens, unpublished manuscript.

6. A similar story appears in E.F. Schumacher, *Good Work* (New York: Harper, 1979), 150-153.

7. See M. Scott Peck, *The Road Less Travelled* (New York: Simon & Schuster, 1978) for an excellent discussion of the work necessary for spiritual discernment and growth.

8. See D.M. Dooling and Paul Jordan Smith, *I Become Part of It* (New York: Paraholm Books 1989) for a discussion of a similar understanding of the power of names in the Navajo culture.

9. The "Johari" window is a helpful picture regarding this dynamic. This window is a grid formed by two rows labelled "self" and "other" and two columns labelled "known" and "unknown." The resulting four-

box grid resembles a window. Self-aware people have a large self/ known "pane" and utilize others to move information from the known/ others "pane" to the known/self "pane," thereby enlarging it.

10. A helpful book is Roy M. Oswald's *How to Build A Support System for Your Ministry* (Washington, DC: The Alban Institute, 1991).

Chapter 3

1. For a very brief explanation, see Carl G. Jung, ed., *Man and His Symbols* (New York: Dell Publishing, 1964), 45-56.

2. David Keirsey and Marilyn Bates, *Please Understand Me: Character and Temperament Types* (Del Mar, CA: Prometheus Nemesis Book Co., 1978).

3. Eric Berne, *Games People Play: the Psychology of Human Relationships* (New York: Grove Press, 1964).

4. For help in changing response transactions and scripts, see also Suzette Haden Elgin, *The Gentle Art of Verbal Self-Defense* (San Diego: Dorsett Press, 1980–also published by Prentice-Hall, Inc,).

5. Mike Ashcraft, "Dealing with Difficult Church Members," *The Five Stones* (Winter, 1987): 2-4.

6. Michael Kroll, "Caring for the Family of God," *The Five Stones* (Fall, 1991): 14.

7. G. Lloyd Rediger, "Clergy Killers," *The Clergy Journal* (August, 1993): 1-2.

8. Michael Kroll, "You Can Prevent Church Killers from Striking Again," *The Five Stones* (Spring, 1992): 14-18.

9. Ashcraft, op.cit.

10. See Anthony G. Pappas, *Entering the World of the Small Church* (Washington, DC: The Alban Institute, 1989).

11. Rediger, op.cit.

Chapter 4

1. Margaret Fletcher Clark, "Ten Models of Ordained Ministry," *Action Information* vol. ix, no. 5 (Nov-Dec 1983).

2. Loren Mead in Clark, ibid.

3. Steve Burt, *Activating Leadership in the Small Church: Clergy and Laity Working Together* (Valley Forge, PA: Judson Press, 1988): 100-103.

4. James M. Acheson, *The Lobster Gangs of Maine* (Hanover, NH: University Press of New England, 1988).

5. Ibid., 59-61.

6. Ibid., 61-62.

7. Ibid., 62.

Chapter 5

1. Arlin J. Routhauge, *Sizing Up Your Congregation for New Member Ministry* (New York: The Episcopal Church Center, 1983).

2. Lyle E. Schaller, *Looking in the Mirror: Self-Appraisal in the Local Church* (Nashville: Abingdon Press, 1984).

3. Anthony G. Pappas, *Entering the World of the Small Church: A Guide for Leaders* (Washington, DC: The Alban Institute, 1988).

4. David R. Ray, *The Big Small Church Book* (Cleveland: The Pilgrim Press, 1992), 1-6.

5. See, for example, the quotations in my article: Anthony G. Pappas, "The Speckled Horse: Three Questions for the Small Church," *American Baptist Quarterly*, vol. xi, no. 1 (March 1992): 41.

6. Loren B. Mead, *More Than Numbers: The Ways Churches Grow* (Bethesda, MD: The Alban Institute, 1993).

7. Loren B. Mead, *The Once and Future Church: Reinventing the Congregation for a New Mission Frontier* (Washington, DC: The Alban Institute, 1991).

8. Thomas Alexander, "Lessons from Portland: Reflections on Small Church Ministry," *The Five Stones* (Winter 1995).

9. So the apocryphal story about the small church pastor who welcomed six new persons into membership only to hear a deacon complain that he hardly knew anyone at church anymore! A more painful real life story is found in Marcia Rickett's article "The Place To Go," *The American Baptist Magazine*, March 1991, 20-21.

10. E.g., Carl Dudley, whose insights into small church dynamics were brilliant and seminal, has chosen for decades to minister in other contexts. Doug Walrath, teacher, mentor, friend, and inspiration to me, chuckles over his modest showing in a mid/large sized church. See Douglas Alan Walrath, *Making It Work: Effective Administration in the Small Church* (Valley Forge, PA: Judson Press, 1994).

11. Larry Gibbons, "Transforming Congregational Culture: An Approach to Change in the Local Church," *The Five Stones* (1989).

12. On the sheet "Some Elements of Church Culture," one or more leaders can rank their congregation between the poles of the spectrum for each of the seven dimensions of congregational culture. This exercise can be useful for discovering a congregation's culture in the following ways:

—Rankings in the middle probably indicate areas of strength and invite exploration as to content.

—Rankings far to the left or right probably indicate areas of weakness that ministry may choose to focus on.

—If there are consistent differences between types of responders (e.g., lay/pastor, new members/old members), the differences may reveal much about the congregation's culture and/or the existence of subcultures.

—Exploration of differences can lead to an informative discussion of the ways in which the congregation is perceived by its members.

13. Samuel C. Heilman, *Synagogue Life: A Study in Symbolic Interaction* (Chicago: University of Chicago Press, 1976). Summarized by Carl Dudley in *The Five Stones* (Summer, 1989): 6.

14. I am indebted to Carl Dudley for much of this analysis.

15. James F. Hopewell, *Congregation Stories and Structures* (Philadelphia: Fortress Press, 1987).

16. Oliver Sachs, *The Man Who Mistook His Wife for a Hat and Other Clinical Tales* (New York: Summit Books, 1985): 22-24.

17. "School Committee Takes Care of Business," *The Block Island Times* (April 30, 1994): 11.

18. Larry Gibbons, "Can Old First Church Change?" *The Five Stones,* vol. 11, no. 2 (Spring, 1993): 7-11.

19. John A. Hostetler, *Amish Society,* 3rd ed. (Baltimore: The Johns Hopkins University Press, 1980).

20. Erik H, Erikson, *Childhood and Society* (New York: W.W. Norton & Co., 1963).

21. Robert D. Dale, *To Dream Again: How to Help Your Church Come Alive* (Nashville: Broadman Press. 1981), 15, 17. Copyright 1981 Broadman Press. All rights reserved. Used by permission.

22. Martin F. Saarinen, *The Life Cycle of a Congregation* (Washington, DC: The Alban Institute, 1986), 22-23.

23. Dale, op.cit, 135.

24. Edwin H. Friedman, *Generation to Generation: Family Process in Church and Synagogue* (New York: The Guilford Press, 1985).

25. Ibid., 229.
26. Ibid., 231.

Chapter 6

1. Carl S. Dudley, *Affectional and Directional Orientations to Faith* (Washington, DC: The Alban Institute, 1982).

2. Ibid., 3-4.

3. Ibid., 11-12.

4. Douglas Alan Walrath, *Frameworks: Patterns of Living and Believing Today* (New York: The Pilgrim Press, 1987). Reprinted by permission of the Pilgrim Press, Cleveland, Ohio.

5. Ibid., 79-80.

6. Douglas Alan Walrath, *Options: How to Develop and Share Christian Faith Today* (New York: The Pilgrim Press, 1988).

7. Walrath, op.cit., 84..

8. Owen D. Owens, *Growing Churches for a New Age* (Valley Forge, PA: Judson Press, 1991). See pages 51-68.

9. See Gary E. Farley, "Becoming an Information Age Church," *The Five Stones*, vol. 11, no. 2 (Spring 1993): 2-5.

10. Tex Sample, *U.S. Lifestyles and Mainline Churches: A Key to Reaching People in the 90's* (Louisville, KY: Westminster/John Knox Press, 1990).

11. L. Shannon Jung, "Review of U.S. Lifestyles and Mainline Churches," *The Five Stones*, vol. 9, no. 1 (Winter 1991), 17-19.

12. Read the whole story in Owen D. Owens' *Growing Churches for a New Age* (Valley Forge, PA: Judson Press, 1981), 51-68.

13. See Walter J. Ong, *Orality and Literacy: the Technologizing of the Word* (New York: Routledge, 1982).

14. Thanks to Doug Walrath for these contrasting characteristics.

15. See Philippians 2 for an alternative attitude!

16. See The Alban Institute's "Once and Future Church" series for a solid beginning in this quest.

The Alban Institute:
an invitation to membership

The Alban Institute, begun in 1974, believes that the congregation is essential to the task of equipping the people of God to minister in the church and the world. A multi-denominational membership organization, the Institute provides on-site training, educational programs, consulting, research, and publishing for hundreds of churches across the country.

The Alban Institute invites you to be a member of this partnership of laity, clergy, and executives–a partnership that brings together people who are raising important questions about congregational life and people who are trying new solutions, making new discoveries, finding a new way of getting clear about the task of ministry. The Institute exists to provide you with the kinds of information and resources you need to support your ministries.

Join us now and enjoy these benefits:

CONGREGATIONS: The Alban Journal, a highly respected journal published six times a year, to keep you up to date on current issues and trends.

Inside Information, Alban's quarterly newsletter, keeps you informed about research and other happenings around Alban. Available to members only.

Publications Discounts:

    ☐ 15% for Individual, Retired Clergy, and Seminarian Members
    ☐ 25% for Congregational Members
    ☐ 40% for Judicatory and Seminary Executive Members

Discounts on Training and Education Events

Write our Membership Department at the address below or call us at 1-800-486-1318 or 301-718-4407 for more information about how to join The Alban Institute's growing membership, particularly about Congregational Membership in which 12 designated persons receive all benefits of membership.

 The Alban Institute, Inc.
Suite 433 North
4550 Montgomery Avenue
Bethesda, MD 20814-3341